Tripping Through the American Night

Ron Jacobs

HANIAN MEDIA

ISBN: 0615481876
ISBN-13: 978-0615481876

For those I met along the way

Names have been changed when necessary to protect
the innocent and not-so-innocent

Some of the material in this book appeared in a slightly
different form in *Counterpunch, Dissident Voice,
Works In Progress,* and *The Vermont Times.* All of the
essays were written between 1999 and 2011.

The Reality That Casts the Shadow

When I was younger I tried on a couple different sectarian ideological costumes and found that, just like my wardrobe (a rather loose definition of the clothes I wear) no particular rigid set of ideologies fits me to a "t." Instead, I have absorbed a multiplicity of left and anarchist theoreticians and, with Marx and Engels as the foundation of them all, have arrived at a critical way of perceiving the world of humans. The essence of the critical framework I use to make sense of the world is that the system of profit is essentially a crooked scheme. This is nowhere more clear than in the United States.

The United States was formed as a capitalist and colonial nation. Since the first ships landed in Jamestown and Plymouth Rock, this nation has been involved in claiming other people's lands and resources for its own. After the establishment of the United States, the land and riches taken from the indigenous peoples became the property of the wealthy classes who were now Americans instead of British. The farmers and workers assumed that they too would share in the spoils. When there was no more land to steal from the natives, purchase from other European nations or take by force on the continent, Washington's eyes looked westward across the seas and intensified their grip on the continent to its south. It was then that the US empire of today got its true beginning. Teddy Roosevelt did more than storm a hill with his rough riders. He made fact the desire of William McKinley and US industry and finance to move the inland empire across the waters. Under the guise of helping the peoples of Cuba and the Philippines their freedom, the United States made them their subjects. From Teddy Roosevelt--who was a progressive and an imperialist to Barack Obama, who is a progressive of today and an imperialist, the legacy continues.

Let's define our terms. To me, imperialism is the process whereby capitalist nations expand into other countries via economic aid, diplomacy, and war in search of raw materials and resources, cheaper labor, and new markets. This expansion is necessary because of the essential nature of capitalism: in order to survive, it must make a profit. In order to make a profit, it must minimize costs, produce ever more goods, and create markets to sell those goods. So, when a country can not provide all of the resources and labor required by a capitalist enterprise (or collection of enterprises) and

2

the markets of that country are saturated with goods, the enterprises move overseas. When necessary, they enlist the government (which is made up of men and women who believe in the holiness of profit) to help them make that move. Hence, so-called free trade deals and wars. Most important to today's empire are the resources that create energy. Washington has proven it will do almost anything to maintain its control over these resources and will fight through whatever means it considers necessary to prevent its competitors from gaining comparable access.

When I moved to Washington state in 1985, I worked in a small electronics assembly plant. The pay was minimum wage ($3.35/hr at the time) but the plant was one of the few places in Shelton to work. Jobs with the Simpson timber company were in a steady decline due in part to the diversification of the company's holding and an accompanying de-emphasis on timber. Many of the workers at the plant were women and young people who supplemented their partner's or parent's unemployment checks.

At the assembly plant we were expected to work fifty to sixty hours a week during busy periods, yet fear layoffs with less than a twenty-four hour warning when

3

work was slow. The managers were pleasant enough, and they worked as many hours (or more) as us hourly workers. At the home plant in Redmond, people did the same type of work for three times as much money. Most of the work, however, was done in Shelton. Obviously, the Shelton plant was opened in order to take advantage of a favorable labor situation. In other words, a depressed economy. Just like in Mexico, South Korea, Central America, and dozens of other places dominated by transnational capital. Little did those of working there at the time realize that our predicament would become not only commonplace, but also federal and international law.

One example of this was the North American Free Trade Agreement (NAFTA). NAFTA was advertised by its proponents as a treaty which encouraged free and equal trade between the US and its hemispheric neighbors. Such trade, went the reasoning, would provide greater employment opportunities for everyone in the affected countries. In reality, the only freedom encouraged by NAFTA is the transnationals' freedom to exploit the people and the lands of those countries more than they do already. The employment provided, if the corporations have their way, would be at lower wages and with even less security than at present. Sure, there might be more jobs, bu there will also be more poverty among those with jobs. As we know, the massive popular movement against NAFTA and the World Trade Organization (WTO) barely changed this trend in modern capitalism. It did, however, cause the architects of this trend to meet under heavy armed guard, provoking massive and militant protests around the world. In other words, the capitalists changed their tactics while keeping their strategy intact. The current economic crisis of capitalism has done more to challenge the world of free trade then most of our protests. Yet, if it weren't for those protests, there would not have been the popular understanding of the true nature of these agreements.

I was sitting on the couch last Saturday evening watching a baseball game with my friend's fourteen year old daughter. My night for childcare, you see. It's not the Red Sox, so I don't care who wins. My child care charge tells me it's a lot more fun for her to watch games with me when the Red Sox aren't playing. Says I don't get as excited one way or the other when they're not playing. No cussing at the television. She's right.

Rationality takes over because I don't care who wins. Anyhow, back to the game.

We're listening to the so-called "color" guy repeat everything the play-by-play announcer says and then add his own take on the just completed selection of pitches. Nowadays FOX Sports--the network that carries most of the big professional sporting contests in the US--add these obnoxious animated features to their explanatory narrative. Some yellow baseball with a face that FOX named Scooter explains various pitches to the uninitiated. Of course, every little extra feature like Scooter is sponsored by some damn corporation. So, the "color" guy says something like: "Let's see what the EXXONMobil Scooter has to say about the Ford Motor Company pitch selection to that last batter....." When he's finished, the play-by-play guy says something like this, "Now, we're going to take this game sponsored by the Army of One and Ameriquest Mortgage to a commercial break. Be right back in a Xanax minute. Now, I don't have the exact corporate sponsors there, but you get the point. One would think it was ever thus.

See, the empire is also in our minds It's not only on FoxSports and FoxNews. It's prevalent in the show 24 and it's in the *New York Times*. It's in Steve

Colbert's shtick for the troops in Iraq in May 2009 and it's in the mindset that has liberals and right wingers honoring the US military for defending our freedom while taking away that of the Iraqis and Afghans. It's in how the discussion about Afghanistan and Somalia is framed and it's obvious as hell in the choices Barack Obama made to run his foreign policy and the nature of that policy since January 2009. We see the nature of the empire when we hear on the news that unemployment rates are climbing while taxpayer money is being spent on bailing out the wealthy and their corporations. If the news talked about the wars, we would also hear about how much money is being poured down those endless drains--drains that epitomize the nature of the empire. A nature that depends on war and its profits to exist. Indeed, an existence that would no longer be without them. So instead of discussions in the media about the cost of these wars in humanity and money, we get discussions about how to run these wars "better." And every enhancement takes more money from education, health and other social services, and props up the unstable, but destructive status quo.

Let's look at other manifestations of that empire of the mind. They include recruiters in your high school.

Camps for kids as young as 10 run by the military that teach them the values required to become the empire's future troops. so whether you are fighting the presence of recruiters in your school or your kids recreational facilities or targeting the high tech mystery bunker in the Nevada desert that sends unmanned drones on killing missions across the world, you are fighting the empire.

Providing intellectual and political support to this system are assumptions by citizens that lie at the heart of what we call American exceptionalism. This idea that the US is somehow operating for different reasons than previous empires--bringing freedom, for women's rights, etc.--is what informs the Washington establishment from Cheney to Obama and from FoxNews to the *Boston Globe*. Now that there is a "liberal" in office it seems more prevalent than it has been since Bill Clinton bombed Yugoslavia in 1999. The movement against Bush's war has become silent now that the wars and occupations have become Obama's.

America is not a better country than any other. Its citizens and residents are as venal and as great as any others in any other part of the world. The only thing that sets us apart is our wealth. The only reason we have that wealth is because we stole it. God didn't give it to us, nor did any greater American intelligence or know-how. Robbery is what our foreign policy is based on, just like our racial policies. It's not the policies that need to change, but the foundation upon which those policies flourish.

We stand at a precipice or we stand at a gateway--a precipice where the world's nations fall into world war as capitalist competition tightens or a gateway to a new world where the world's peoples embrace a policy of internationalism and refuse to join a competition that seems only too likely to end in an even greater war than the relative wildfires of war already unleashed. I don't know if what I have written over the past several years makes a difference in our understanding of the world and what needs to be done to make it survivable in the future. More importantly, I don't know if I might have better spent my time focusing solely on organizing. However, one does what one can until one has to do what one must. By this I mean that I wrote when my employment and family situation made the effort of all-out organizing too difficult to manage. However, when a war was threatened or a racist incident occurred that required more of an organizing effort, then it was time for me to do what I felt I must do, no matter what the effect on my employment status or even my family. Fortunately, neither suffered to a point that made them irretrievable. That can not be said for everyone involved in fighting the imperial beast. All too many have lost their lives. Plenty more have lost their jobs and endangered their relationships with their loved ones.

This, then, is the framework from which the essays in this book have been written. The myth that is the United States is one whose strength is ever more frayed. Yet, the denial of this weakness insures its continuation no matter what the cost.

Television, Murder and Vietnam

I was a kid in 1968. It was the year I turned 13 and it was the year my dad began to prepare to go to Vietnam. The Tet offensive was on the television in January. The picture of the South Vietnamese police chief killing a suspected NLF fighter shook up our dinner table the night it was in the news. After that, my father didn't watch television news when his younger kids were around. I won grand prize in the science fair at my junior high for an investigation into whether or not my pet guppies talked. Then I won first place in my division at the statewide fair held the last weekend in March of that year at the University of Maryland's Cole Field House.

My dad picked me up after the fair closed down. After we had packed the exhibit in the trunk of his station wagon, we got in the front seat. On the way from College Park, MD to our house in Laurel, MD-about ten miles away-we listened to the speech by President Johnson where he told the nation that he would not "seek or accept the nomination" for his party's candidacy for the presidency. After a brief discussion with my dad about what this meant and why it happened, we turned to a conversation about the differences between FM and AM radio. Then he told me that he had been given orders to go to Vietnam. I didn't say anything while he told me when he thought he would be leaving and what it meant for the family. He never mentioned whether he thought what he would be doing there was right or wrong. When we got home, I talked with my parents for a few minutes and went to bed.

The next day in Social Studies class the teacher talked about how remarkable it was that Lyndon Johnson had decided not to run for reelection. From there, he segued into a conversation about the elections. After a quick show of hands regarding who we supported, he asked me why I supported Gene McCarthy. I told him it was because he wanted to end the war in Vietnam. In fact, McCarthy was calling for a negotiated settlement with the northern Vietnamese and the NLF while everyone else (except for maybe Bobby Kennedy) was still talking about some kind of victory. There was only one other person in the class who supported McCarthy. Two or three others supported Bobby Kennedy, who had entered the race only days before. Most supported either Humphrey (who was LBJ's replacement) or Nixon. On the playground at lunch that day, one of the Nixon supporters called me a faggot because I supported McCarthy.

Three days later, April 4, 1968, I was watching TV with my older sister when the graphic before a breaking news bulletin flashed across the screen. I walked over to the TV and turned up the volume. (There were no remotes back then.) A talking head came on the screen and announced that Martin Luther King, Jr. had been shot in Memphis. My sister and I looked at each other. We knew this was something big. I sat down to watch the incoming news while my sister put our younger siblings to bed. I knew that King had been in Memphis supporting a strike of sanitation workers and that there had been trouble at one of the marches. When our parents got home, I told my father what had happened. He sat down for a few minutes and watched as news reports filtered in about angry blacks gathering in different parts of Washington, DC. That night, I listened to WTOP--the all news station in DC-- relay reports on the growing insurrection in that city and around the nation. When I got up to deliver my newspaper route the next morning, the front page was covered with banner headlines and full color pictures of the assassination and the angry response.

The following week, our family attended a cookout at a neighbor's house down the block in our lily-white middle class suburban development. Most of Maryland was under curfew, gun sales were forbidden and liquor sales had been stopped in DC, Baltimore and several counties. While I ate beans, salad and burgers from the paper plate I had loaded up, some of the adults conversed about the murder and the insurrection. The remarks I heard from some of the neighbors changed my impression of them forever. I had never heard such racist remarks before except from some of the working class toughs who wore their hair greased back like early Elvis and smoked cigarettes while hanging out in front of the Peoples Drug Store at the local shopping center. If I learned one thing that night, it was that the ignorance of racism knew no class boundaries. The names they called Martin Luther King and the suggestions they had for the local police to "keep order" in the black section of town were reminiscent of the Klan literature one of my newspaper customers gave me almost every time I collected his month's payment from him. Literature that I threw away after reading it the first time and being repulsed by the hatred therein.

After the King assassination I began to read the newspaper much more carefully. Not just the sports section like before, but all of the news sections as well. Prior to that, I had skimmed the front page and the local section, but had never really read anything too carefully. As the presidential campaign heated up, I switched my allegiance to Bobby Kennedy. His ability to gather huge crowds no matter where he showed up-West Virginia one day and Washington, DC the next-was impressive. He had somehow figured out how to speak to people on a different level than all of the other candidates and he said he was against the war. Meanwhile, I had discovered another newspaper that told a completely different story. That paper was Washington DC's first underground paper, The Washington Free Press. A friend's older brother who went to the University of Maryland used to give me his old copies when he was done with them. Somewhere not very far from the boring suburban redneck town that I lived in there was something going on that was both new and connected to the revolution I was certain had to be happening somewhere. It had to be happening because the Beatles were singing about it, the Rolling Stones seemed to have joined it, and the *Free Press* reported it. I didn't understand why they didn't like Kennedy or thought the elections were bullshit but I wanted to find out why.

When Bobby Kennedy was killed I was watching TV with my sister once again. I remember feeling angry, sad and bitter all at the same time. After he was killed I gave up on the elections for a while. No more passing out campaign literature at the shopping center or door to door. There was nothing left to do but wait until the convention and hope some kind of miracle happened that would stop the war. A war my dad was heading off to in a few short months. In late July we took a family vacation at a beach near Norfolk, VA. My father was getting ready to go to some kind of school there that was required before he went away to Vietnam. The name of that school? Air War College. You don't have to guess what the general course of studies was. After a week, my older sister and I returned to Laurel. I delivered my newspapers, mowed lawns for the neighbors and hung out with my friends listening to music, reading, and watching TV. It was one of those nights of TV watching when another news bulletin flashed across the screen. Soviet troops had invaded Czechoslovakia. This was a year for news bulletins. I followed this event with interest because I was secretly hoping that the Czechs truly could find some kind of humane alternative to both Stalinism and monopoly capitalism, even if that terminology was unknown to me at the time.

Not long after that night, I began watching the coverage of the Democratic Convention in Chicago. I recall a sign shown on television that said "Welcome to Czechago." Those few nights of watching cops beat the shit out of people and politicians showing their true colors-be they fascist in nature or on the side of the protesters-did more to educate and radicalize me than pretty much anything I had ever read or would ever read in my life. The angry repartee between William F. Buckley, Jr. and Gore Vidal on one of the networks gelled in my mind along with pictures of tear gas, bloodied reporters, people chanting "The whole world's watching," and my mom crying because her country was falling to pieces. When my dad came home for a weekend, he tried to convince me that the protesters were wrong and that voting was the way to solve the country's problems. I was not convinced.

By this time, Detroit Tigers pitcher Denny McLain was getting closer and closer to a mark not reached by a major league pitcher in many seasons. He was approaching thirty wins. Although I had given my heart to the Red Sox the year before, I tried to watch or listen to every game McLain pitched. If it wasn't on TV and I couldn't get the game over my AM radio via the nighttime skip phenomenon that somehow brought the games to my transistor, then I reconstructed the box scores the next morning before I delivered my papers. When the World Series came around, I was pulling for Bob Gibson and the St. Louis Cardinals. I loved to watch Gibson pitch even though he had beat the Red Sox the year before.

Meanwhile, in school we were composing a scrapbook for the elections. Each of us had to choose either Nixon or Humphrey for our scrapbook and fill it with materials related to the campaign. I chose Humphrey, even though he was for the war, he wasn't Nixon. When it came time to turn in the scrapbook, I covered the front of the binder with "Dick Gregory for President" stickers. My teacher was not happy. She yelled at me and asked how I could support someone who opposed the war when my dad was on his way over there. I snidely suggested that the answer was obvious and ended up being sent to the counselor. He yelled at me and told me to get my head out of my ass. I left there thinking that he should do the same.

On election day we watched the final returns come in over the television in our social studies class. There weren't any exit poll projections back then. The news people actually let the election run its course. When Walter Cronkite said that Nixon had won I had a feeling that the world as I knew it was over. In fact, it was only getting worse. The difference was now I was aware of it. I didn't hit the streets in protest for another year but I was already there in my heart and soul.

Hypocrites, Pharisees and Martin Luther King, Jr.

April 4, 1968. I was watching TV that Thursday night when a bulletin flashed across the screen . Martin Luther King Jr. was dead, shot dead in Memphis. By the time I woke up the next morning to deliver papers, cities were on fire across the land. As I delivered the Washington Post to the customers on my route in the Maryland suburb that I lived in, I tried to make some sense of the storm. At school, my social studies teacher, a young guy who was teaching us about Karl Marx, said a few words over the public address system about the senseless and tragic murder The black kids seemed distant and some of the more racist white kids (those who wore their Wallace for President buttons to school), gleeful. I just wished there was something I could do.

In church that Sunday, the priest read a letter from the archbishop expressing sorrow at the assassination and the violent response it had wrought. His letter urged each and every one of us to pray and, additionally, contribute food and clothing to those who had been left homeless as a result of the revolt in the cities. My mother and I volunteered to join in a door-to-door collection campaign.

That Sunday afternoon we began. Mom waited in the car while a friend and I knocked on doors asking for a can or two of food. Everyone who was home offered something even if it was just a can of peas. We had covered about half of our neighborhood and the station wagon was more than half full. My teenage faith in humanity was restored.

Then I knocked on the next door. This house belonged to a man whose daughter sat next to me in English class. He owned a construction business and had always been nice to me. I knocked again His daughter came to the door. She said hi . I answered in kind and told her my purpose. She headed to the kitchen for some canned goods. On her way back with a couple cans her dad came into the front room. He nodded hello and asked me what I was up to. Collecting food for the people made homeless by the riots, I replied. His daughter proceeded to drop the cans she held into the bag I was carrying. I thanked her and turned around to leave.

"Wait a goddam minute!" yelled her dad. I turned around in shock.

"Yes sir?" I questioned.

"None of my food is going to them niggers," he continued yelling. "Let 'em all die."

I couldn't believe my ears. This man was a Catholic like me. He believed in Jesus and Jesus said to love your neighbor as yourself. But sir, I began. Give me back my food and get out of here, you niggerlover, he shouted. And stay away from my daughter. His daughter had already left the room in tears. I left shaking, not believing what had happened,

A couple months later, Bobby Kennedy was dead too. He'd been my choice for president. The funeral was on television and the train came through our town. I wanted to go down to the track to pay my respects, but was afraid to ask my dad. He had never expressed much like for the Kennedys and Bobby was probably his least favorite, although thirty years later he said he probably would have voted for him. My mom, on the other hand, was enthralled by the family. We settled for watching the proceedings on TV.

As we know, since that day in April 1968, Martin Luther King has become a virtual saint, with all that such a signifier connotes. Men and women of all political stripes take his name in vain. Warmakers and racists quote him as if the words he wrote in opposition to their world were written for them and not to them. As if it was the poor and the non-white who were King's nemesis and not the rich and powerful and their police. These people have much more use for him as a dead man than they ever did when he was alive. Don't fall for their lies.

Tears of Rage: Remembering May 1970

One of the most hopeful aspects of the 2003-2007 movement against the war is the large numbers of young people who are not only involved, but are taking the initiative. In our local coalition here in Vermont, the high school and college students (and those of that age who are not in school) have involved themselves in most of the planning and strategizing. To their credit, most of the older folks have encouraged this and invited these coalition members' input. As a person who opposed the US war in Vietnam while in high school, my empathy for today's younger protestors stems from the frustration I felt when ignored by older activists merely because of my age. Indeed, the only antiwarriors who encouraged me to write and organize back in the early 1970s were the GIs who I hung out with in Germany.

As the month of May rolls around again, I am reminded of two dates from that month: May 4th and May 14th. These are the anniversaries of the 1970 murders of student antiwar protestors at Kent State University in Ohio and Jackson State College in Mississippi by military and lawmen. These murders marked a turning point in the war and the protest against it. The antiwar movement grew up with those murders. Now, protest meant risking one's life. The U.S. government had made it clear once and for all that it would tolerate only so much dissent. Of course, African-American and other protesters of color-and the revolutionary anti-imperialist wing of the antiwar movement-had known this all along. After the original burst of anger that brought millions into the streets and shut down universities and high schools around the country, many protesters put away their banners and raised fists for a life with less confrontation. The rest of us reaffirmed our commitment to do whatever it took to stop the war.

Despite its relatively short life, the current movement against the war and whatever else lies ahead is in its adolescence. We share an innocence with that pre-May 1970 movement, yet at the same time know that the state is willing to do whatever it takes to keep its power and its wars. Messrs. Bush, Ashcroft, and Rumsfeld have left us no doubt in that regard. We have yet to see police or army murders of protesters in the US this time around, although two Western members of the international movement have been killed by the Israeli military in the last couple of months (and a third mortally wounded).

I've jotted down some memories from those days in early May 1970. My dad returned from DaNang, Vietnam in February of that year, where he had spent the previous year as an officer in the Air Force. I had become more opposed to the war during that same time. I was in ninth grade. Dad came back in February of 1970. Although I was glad to see him out of harm's way, there were times I wished I was somewhere else.

We arrived in Frankfurt am Main in March 1970. Within a week, my siblings and I were back in school. The junior high I attended was on the other side of the city on a military compound. It had been a German women's prison prior to its utilization as a school. The school building was surrounded by a twelve foot high wall. Each of its corners held an empty guard tower. Most of the students felt that prison was an appropriate metaphor for their experiences there. I made a few friends pretty quickly.

This always happened on military bases since most of the students were always in transit, but the fact that I owned some rock records that hadn't made it to the Post Exchange or into the German music stores certainly helped. With most students feeling that the epicenter of our (counter)culture lay in the U.S., anyone who arrived from the States and was just a little bit hip was milked for updates on what was really happening. Neither the Stars & Stripes newspaper nor the Armed Forces Radio Network were providing that kind of news. The only news the Stars and Stripes was really good for was sports news, and that wasn't something I discussed with my new counterculture friends.

When I awoke on May 1 that year, I was, like many other people in the world, incredulous and pissed off that Nixon had sent troops into Cambodia. Although my political awareness was still relatively unformed, it had taken me no time to realize that Richard Nixon was a pig. Still, I didn't think he or anyone else would actually expand the war in Southeast Asia when everybody-- including my dad--wanted it to end. When I went to the kitchen for breakfast my father was still there and we had a short debate about the invasion before he headed off to work. That interaction got me fired up for a day of debate. Sure enough, even though homeroom was run by the gym teacher (a man with the last name of Agnew who usually didn't talk about anything other than sports), we spent the whole class period arguing about the war. By the time civics class came up right before lunch, some of the more radical students (whom I was just beginning to know) were trying to organize some kind of protest. However, since the weekend was coming up, nothing concrete was devised.

When we got back to school on Monday, May 4, most of us who cared had heard the news reports all weekend about the massive protests taking place all over the US against Nixon's move into Cambodia. In addition, the German students had kept the police busy all weekend in Frankfurt with constant rallies and marches against the invasion, of which I attended at least one. By noon on Monday, some hastily drawn posters began appearing on the walls of our junior high urging students to protest the war on Wednesday, May 6, by wearing black armbands and refusing to go to homeroom. Of course, as soon as the posters appeared, they were ripped down by administrators or a pro-war student or teacher. One girl was suspended when she refused to remove a poster she had just put up. That night I found some black material and made myself an armband.

Like always, I turned on the radio when I awoke the next morning, May 5th. I liked to listen to the news, especially when something big was happening. I was not prepared, however, for the news that morning. Nor do I think I will ever forget how I felt when I first heard it. Four students had been shot dead in Kent, Ohio by the National Guard while protesting the war. Several others were injured. I knew what Dylan meant when he sang of his tears of rage. My eyes were brimming over with such tears and my heart was pounding in anger and disbelief. I didn't say much as I got ready for school. My mom was silent as I read the Stars and Stripes report on the killings over Cheerios. My older sister and I talked about them while we ate.

I put my armband on while waiting for the school bus. Upon arriving at school, I searched for some of the kids most involved in the antiwar planning. In homeroom, Mr. Agnew read a memo from the principal expressing regret over the slayings in Ohio, but warned that no protest of any kind would be allowed at Frankfurt American Junior High School. The gym teacher (who I was beginning to believe opposed the war as much as I did) looked around, noting that three or four of us wore black armbands, and said nothing. One of the guys asked if he could read something relevant to the current events and the teacher said yes. Steve took out a copy of the text to Arlo Guthrie's antiwar poem "Alice's Restaurant Massacree" and began reading, complete with four-part harmony. By the time he finished, class was over.

Most of the teachers turned the classroom time that day into a discussion of the war in Vietnam and the repression of the movement against it. Those students who wanted to do more than just wear armbands passed the word that people should still refuse to go to homeroom the following day. We would hold a silent vigil in the parking lot instead. A few students were forced to remove their armbands by the more reactionary teachers. Other teachers took armbands provided by the students and wore them themselves, probably risking a pay raise if not their jobs, especially seeing as how the school was on a military base.

When the bell signaling the beginning of classes rang Wednesday morning, about a hundred students in the parking lot made no moves toward the building. We waited for a signal of some kind from one of the protest organizers. As we milled around, certain teachers known for their allegiance to the rules appeared on the outskirts of our small crowd. Slowly but surely they herded us towards the entrance doors and slowly but surely we filed in. I don't think we had a failure of will as much as we had no organization. Later that day there was a two-hour all-school assembly where, after some sanctimonious nonsense from the principal and an Army officer about defending freedom (both of whom were eventually shouted down), we argued about the war. By the time the Jackson State murders took place on May 14th, there was no more arguing left to do. And tears were not enough.

The Day Nixon Was Gone: In Memory of Deep Throat

Little had changed overnight. The war continued in Vietnam. Another southern Vietnamese town had been taken over by the popular forces over the weekend. I left work at 2 in the morning on August 8, 1974 and headed home to sleep. After waking around 10 the same morning, I hitchhiked into Washington, DC. Something big was in the air. The Congressional committees involved in deciding whether or not to impeach Richard Nixon had been meeting all summer. The noose was tightening around the son of a bitch. Word on the street was that Nixon was going to quit. Maybe today, August 8, 1974. His last supporters in Congress were jumping the proverbial ship like the rats that they were. The radio playing on the last ride I caught-from College Park into Georgetown-was playing Bob Dylan's song, "It's All Over Now, Baby Blue."

All summer much of the nation had been riveted to the various congressional hearings devoted to uncovering Nixon's crimes. The theater had been excellent and it looked like the ending was going to be better than anything Hollywood could dream up. It looked like Nixon was going down. Of course, there was an underlying fear that he would declare martial law for the "good of the country" and not go anywhere, but that sentiment was held mostly by leftists. It's not that they didn't have good reason for such fears, given the counterintelligence program that had been conducted against them-a program that intensified under Nixon. But, one hoped that even Nixon had enough respect for his situation to realize when it was time to say goodbye.

I got out of the car at Wisconsin and M Streets and began walking towards the Mall. I wanted to see what was up amongst the Yippies and others who had been hanging around near the seat of power for the past few days in hopes that they would have a resignation or impeachment to celebrate soon. Plus, if the weather got too hot and muggy, I would be near the Smithsonian buildings and their air conditioning. I stopped at a small shop and bought some coffee in a styrofoam cup, then headed on down the street. An hour or so later I was looking at the Capitol Building. Tourists were milling around along with various pro and anti-Nixon elements. Some rightwing preacher was leading a small prayer session and the Yippies were lighting up joints wrapped in American flag rolling papers.

The charges being considered against Mr. Nixon were related to his actions involving the cover-up and obstruction of justice in the matter of the break-in at the Democratic National Committee's Watergate offices; the use of various federal agencies including the FBI, the IRS, and the Secret Service to spy on and otherwise violate the constitutional rights of US citizens; and his failure to respect various subpoenas and requests by the Congress for papers and tape recordings, thereby subverting the constitution of the United States. Another article that had been considered, but was dropped when the writers realized that they would not have enough votes to pass it concerned the secret bombing of Cambodia that Nixon began in 1969 and continued for over a year before the public knew. One can assume this latter charge was too controversial for most of the committee and Congress and was left off the articles of impeachment for fear that it would diminish the case against Nixon. More importantly, the charge regarding the secret bombing was a question of foreign policy and not even the acrimonious 93rd Congress was willing to challenge the president on the Empire's perceived need to be able to bomb when and where it wanted.

Rumor holds that one of the staffers who had researched the Cambodian bombing article and presumably lobbied hard for its inclusion in the final draft of the Article of Impeachment was a young woman named Hilary Clinton. Hard to believe in 2004, isn't it? What happened to her principles? Lost in the wash of opportunism and politics-as-usual, just like those of her husband's and so many others from that time. On the other side of the spectrum, meanwhile, we are provided with George Bush, Dick Cheney, and Donald Rumsfeld, all of who were around when Nixon was going down. Indeed, Cheney and Rumsfeld were already in Washington. George was still out of the circle, preferring drinking and other forms of partying to the serious work of taking over the country. One assumes they learned an important thing or two from watching their president twist slowly in the wind. Lesson one, make certain that you don't get caught and; two, if something is illegal; make it legal before you do it. That way, there is nothing the law can get you on. After all, the current administration ignores subpoenas, conducts secret military operations and violates citizens' constitutional rights with regularity and it's all legal. We can thank the foresight of the Bush administration's predecessors and the perpetually compliant Congress for this scenario.

What did Watergate (the affair, not the building) mean? Was it really business as usual, with the only difference being that Nixon and his men got caught? Or was it something more fundamental to the system of government our leaders like to trumpet to others around the world as being better than any other? I think that the Weather Underground actually had the best take on the whole slimy situation when they wrote in their manifesto Prairie Fire-The Politics of Revolutionary Anti-Imperialism:

> "Watergate is a domestic reflection of the empire in crisis. Every aspect of the prosecution of the Watergate crisis itself remains in the hands of the ruling class. The Watergate investigations observe gentlemanly limits: they have never explored Nixon's deliberate aggression against Black, Chicano, and Puerto Rican communities. Power in the US is a white gentleman's club.
>
> Yet the crisis runs away. It has become the political expression of a process that began in the 1960s-the defeat of the American myth of freedom and democracy."

However, most Americans didn't share Weather's (or the rest of the Left's) cynicism about the true nature of the US system, and were more likely to believe that it was Nixon that was the problem, not the system itself. Objectively, I would argue that history has proven otherwise, but such an argument would still be a hard sell.

As I hung out in the shadow of the Capitol, with Abe Lincoln sitting in massive marbleized judgment at the other end of the Mall, I recalled an April a little more than a year before. I was on the Mall along with perhaps 100,000 other folks demanding the impeachment and trial of Mr. Nixon for the crimes with which he was now going to be charged. After the first few speakers, I had run with perhaps 10,000 others over to the Justice Department, where we threw epithets at the building and the police surrounding it before they chased us away with their clubs and their gas. Now I was on my way to Lafayette Park across from the White House to sit in on what amounted to a political deathwatch.

At Lafayette Park the major media outlets were setting up their equipment trucks. Dan Rather had a choice seat in the park underneath a big tent full of monitors and other equipment. He was not broadcasting as far as I could tell, but joking with the techies. I recalled his exchange with Nixon at a press conference not too many months before:

> Rather: Mr. President, you have lambasted the television networks pretty well. Could I ask you, at the risk of reopening an obvious wound, you say after you have put on a lot of heat that you don't blame anyone. I find that a little puzzling. What is it about the television coverage of you in these past weeks and months that has so aroused your anger?
> Nixon: Don't get the impression that you arouse my anger. (Laughter)
> Rather: I'm afraid, sir, that I have that impression. (Laughter)
> Nixon: You see, one can only be angry with those he respects.

This exchange was but one of many between Rather and Nixon. It had ratcheted up my respect for Mr. Rather and the mainstream press in general. Too bad that respect is almost gone today.

As the afternoon wore on and the heat index rose both in terms of temperature and in anticipation of the upcoming announcement, the park in front of the White House took on a bit of a picnic feeling. I had my Italian hero sandwich and beer. The Yippies were passing out sandwiches made from food they had dumpster-dived and other citizens were sharing sodas, wine, and food. There were some Nixon supporters in the crowd who attempted to make their presence known despite the ridicule they were subjected to. As night settled in, most of them drifted away to share their sorrows with more sympathetic souls.

As the moment approached there was a feeling of apprehension and exhilaration in the air. I was still afraid that Nixon was going to pull a fast one and declare not that he was resigning, but that he was declaring martial law. Than, a few minutes before 9 PM, Dan Rather intoned words that went something like, "Ladies and gentleman, the president of the United States..."

Nixon went on for a minute or two. I joined the crowd around a man who held a transistor radio broadcasting the speech in the air, waiting for the magic words: "Therefore, I shall resign the Presidency effective at noon tomorrow. Vice President Ford will be sworn in as President at that hour in this office." A cheer ran through the crowd. Someone near me popped a cork on the champagne bottle they had purchased just for this moment. Nixon was gone!

The next morning I sat in my parents' house back in Maryland. The nation was nursing its Nixon hangover and the television stations were showing the man and his family on the White House lawn getting ready to board a helicopter. My mom's friend and neighbor-an Irish-American woman whose IRA father had escaped from Ireland in the wake of the Easter Rising in 1916-came in the door without donuts and coffee. She looked at me and smiled. "Got rid of the bastard, eh, Ron?" She said in her best South Boston accent. My mom looked at us both high-fiving each other and said, "It's a sad day for America."

Nowadays, high school history books tell students that the Watergate episode and Nixon's resignation prove that the US way of government works. Personally, I think that the real indicator of how (and for whom) the system works is Gerald Ford's pardon of the man the following month.

Sandwiches and Car Bombs

While I was at the University of Maryland during the 1974-1975 academic year one of the projects among the leftist counterculture community was supporting a group of students who wanted to start a food co-op on campus. These folks were constantly being threatened by an administration that had sold its soul to big business years before.

In this particular instance, the co-op workers had been arrested twice for selling food in front of the student union without a permit. Of course the reason they were selling without a permit was because the school wouldn't give them one because it violated the standard exclusive contract that the Marriot Corporation had with the University. So, the University sent its cops out to cuff a bunch of hippies selling sandwiches. Such obvious corporate buttkissing eventually worked against the school and, after a spring of demonstrations and arrests, the trustees changed the food service contract, and allowed the co-op to operate legally, even giving it a room in the Student Union building and some money to bring their operation up to code.

Later on that year while the co-op struggle languished in officialdom, our cadre of the Revolutionary Student Brigade (RSB) set up a human blockade around a pair of Marines who were attempting to recruit a few good men from the campus. This was the first time since before the Cambodia/Kent State riots in 1970 that any type of military recruitment had been attempted on the University of Maryland campus. Our goal was to make them leave. Every day at noon a bunch of antiwar types would sit down in front of the Marines' table in front of the Student Union building and link arms. Eventually there would be between fifty and a hundred folks completely surrounding the table. The Marines just stood there at attention, but occasionally right wing students, usually big white guys, would charge through the crowd. It wasn't that they wanted to join the Marines --they just wanted to kick some commie butt. From what I remember, the only butt they kicked belonged to a woman with real long hair who attended RSB meetings. One afternoon, she threw her ninety-pound body in front of some guy who thought he was running through the defensive front line of the Washington Redskins football team and he trampled her. She ended up with some badly bruised ribs and a charge of assault. He ended up feeling like a man. After this incident the University had the Marines move inside the Student Union building to a room that was towards the back of the building. They left the campus when nobody cared enough to find them. Before that occurred, however, two of our cadre members from off-campus were arrested on trespassing charges for sitting inside the room where the Marines were. The rest of our cadre and some supporters took over one of the dean's offices and held it until they were released.

One of our other projects was helping to bring down the Shah of Iran-a brutal dictator who was owned lock, stock and barrel by the CIA and the oil companies. His secret police the SAVAK were notorious for the regime of fear they had created in Iran and amongst Iranians around the globe. Lots of Iranian youth studied in the United States, and the DC area certainly had its share. I was one of the liaisons to the Iranian Students Organization ISA. We spent several afternoons together at a crowded office in downtown DC taking part in meetings planning for the upcoming visit to DC by the shah. In return for our support, local ISA members attending the University of Maryland helped us out as much as possible. Once when we were picketing the Administration building over a planned budget cut aimed at the Ethnic Studies department, two Iranian guys driving a black Mercedes pulled up on the sidewalk, jumped out of the car and attacked our Iranian friend whom I'll call Rashif. They almost had him in the car before we realized that they were probably part of the Shah's secret police (SAVAK) and trying to kidnap him. After a bit of a struggle, we managed to rescue him. Rashif was a very dedicated Marxist revolutionary and took it all in stride. It was his instruction that helped me to understand some of the finer nuances of Lenin's treatise on imperialism. After the attack, he disappeared for a couple weeks and then reappeared. After the Iranian revolution I heard that he had returned to Iran. For all I know, Khomeini's soldiers killed him.

While working on the co-op protests at the university, I was reminded that sandwiches had figured into a protest back in high school also. After the Department of Defense School System (which ran all schools on military bases overseas, where my dad was stationed as an Air Force officer) raised prices on all of the cafeteria food back in 1972, some of us asked why.

The answer given by the school administration was that the pentagon had to cut expenses. Our immediate response was why not end the war instead of raising food prices? After all, one fuckin' bomb cost a hell of a lot more money than a high school lunch. A fellow student, TW, and I got together with a few friends and printed a leaflet that asked that very question and announced a lunch boycott until prices were lowered. We gave away sandwiches outside the cafeteria for three days and had speakers talking about everything from the war to David Bowie. A local rock band attempted to give a free concert but was denied electricity by the administration. The boycott was successful for a few days and then lost momentum. People just got tired of making sandwiches and coffee. Prices never went down.

While we boycotted lunch, the revolutionary armed cells of the Red Army Fraktion (RAF) were blowing up U.S. Army buildings. I was at home the evening the first bombs of their campaign destroyed a good portion of the Officers' Club and a part of the IG Farben office building in Frankfurt am Main where hundreds of military folks, including my dad, worked, killing an army colonel. The following morning the US military was very nervous and under a state of high alert.

Military policemen inspected our bags before we left the school bus, and soldiers with small arms stood at several key intersections in the areas of the city where the Americans lived and worked. In the coming weeks, these areas, which had been relatively open, were closed off. Sentry posts were hastily constructed and concrete barriers put in place. Metal detectors were placed in the entrances to U.S. office buildings and military identification cards were scrutinized more closely before one entered buildings like the commissary and Post Exchange.

In the weeks that followed, other bombs were set off in other cities in West Germany. In Heidelberg two GIs were killed when their cars exploded. Apparently, the bombers had placed the bombs under the vehicles unbeknownst to the servicemen. Although I was sympathetic to the reasons behind the bombings, I did not understand or support the murders. It was too simple to blame anybody connected to the military for US imperialism and not take into account the reasons those individuals might be in the service. Of course, the RAF did not really concern itself with those reasons; they just opposed and hated the existence and presence of the US military on foreign soil. So they killed people, more for their own satisfaction than to further the revolution. Sometime around this period a group of friends and I went to a big demonstration in downtown Frankfurt opposing the intensified U.S. bombing of Vietnam and, in the United States, the Weather Underground set off a bomb in the Pentagon.

In mid-June one of the leaders of the RAF-- Andreas Baader--was captured in an apartment near the building where Armed Forces radio was headquartered. This ended the bombings for a while. The buildup towards a police state continued, however. In their search for the remaining members of the RAF, German police set up unannounced roadblocks on the autobahn and stopped every vehicle. Leftist demonstrations were more tightly controlled and the police were freer in their attacks on such protests. In addition, the numbers of police outside rock concerts and festivals increased.

I'm not selling sandwiches these days, but the equation we considered back in high school still works. The cost of the latest imperial war is causing many US residents to go hungry. The rest of us are paying more for our sandwiches and everything else because of the money going to the war and occupation. Some of the costs are direct-less money for so-called safety net expenditures and more for the costs of war; and some are indirect-we pay more for fuel at home, in our cars, and at the grocery store because of shippers' fuel costs rising. And car bombs have become a daily occurrence.

Flashback to the End of a War That Really Did End

April 30, 1975. The war was over. Really over. This wasn't like the peace treaty all the leaders signed in 1973 that didn't really end anything. No, this time it was over. The television in the University of Maryland Student Union showed video footage of helicopters leaving the U.S. embassy roof with a few remaining GIs and other Americans inside while Vietnamese hung on to the sides. Meanwhile the Vietnamese whose side had won were celebrating the entry of NLF and Hanoi forces into Saigon, which was now Ho Chi Minh City.

My friends and I were exhilarated. A war we had known most of our lives was over. A war which seemed an adventure when I was a young boy playing Little League baseball and war games and had become a source of fear and anger as I grew older. A war which took friends of mine and killed some, made others killers and zombies, and forced all of us to grow up before we were ready. A war which took my father away from my family for over a year and had us wondering every day whether he would come back. And had me wondering if my brothers and I would have to go also. A war which showed Americans what America was

49

really about. An America which wasn't pretty, or even honorable. A war which I had begun opposing as a 13-year old by flashing a peace sign and singing "Give Peace a Chance" while my dad was in Danang, and ended up celebrating the victory of America's enemy.

The night of the Vietnamese victory, Pat M. and I invited ourselves to a Student Association-sponsored banquet at the University of Maryland. Pat was a friend and reasonably well-known on campus as a rabble rouser. He had recently begun attending meetings of the radical group I was associated with--the Revolutionary Student Brigades. Once he and I realized we shared a fondness for pot and a passionate dislike of the system, we began to spend lots of time stirring things up. Our roles as campus instigators had made us friends with the more radical elements in the student government which was run by a member of Youth Against War and Fascism at the time. Consequently, we were often invited to members-only functions. If we weren't, most of the time we went anyway.

As for this particular dinner, the food was good, but the wine was better. So much better, in fact, we lifted a half dozen bottles during the post dinner speeches and headed out to the streets to celebrate. On our way to

Route 1 and the strip of bars immediately off the University of Maryland campus we stopped at a friend's dorm room and drew up a banner reading, "Long Live the People of Vietnam", and scored a couple tabs of acid and a corkscrew. After all, this antiwar movement was about more than Washington's war against the Vietnamese. It was a war of its own against the consciousness that started the war in the first place. John Foster Dulles, Richard Nixon, LBJ. The fear of communism, sexuality and marijuana. Many of us against Washington's war for empire were fighting another war to make our world a place where fear took a backseat to joy.

By the time we made it to the street the acid was edging out the fog of the alcohol and providing a nice clarity to the night. Pat and I opened a bottle of wine each, spread out our banner, and shouted some revolutionary slogans about Ho Chi Minh and so on. After a half hour or so, another thirty people had joined us. By then we were spilling into the streets, drinking wine and smoking weed. Of course, the police showed up.

The funny thing was, they didn't do much. After asking us what was going on, they told us to stay out of the road and drove off. I'm still not sure what Pat and I told them but, whatever it was, it worked. In retrospect, I put it among those moments where the clarity of psychedelic thought patterns befuddles the linear thinker, the authoritarian, so much that they just don't want to bother with figuring it out. So, instead, they left it alone and hoped we would just go away. Later, we headed into DC to celebrate with a few hundred other antiwarriors.

A couple weeks later, Gerald Ford ordered an attack on Cambodia after the merchant ship Mayaquez was seized and released. A final flurry of killing from a vanquished nation. A decade later, Ronald Reagan was heralding CIA-funded right-wing contras in Nicaragua and Islamic mujahedin in Afghanistan.

Now US soldiers fight the mujahedin's progeny in a war that guarantees its continuation as surely as it spawns another generation of hate. The forces represented by Reagan were the beginning of a long march back to the world that the antiwar movement and counterculture thought it could change. It's not that I'm saying (nor am I convinced) that the forces of linearity and authoritarianism have regained the control they had before the 1960s. However, they certainly have learned how to accommodate and neutralize those strains in the US political and cultural spheres that challenged them so headily back then.

The Democratic Party, which funds every war that comes along whether it started under their watch or not, has become what stands for an antiwar movement in the US.   Meanwhile, in the United States, the real opposition to imperial war speaks to an audience deafened by the false hope of an Obama nation.

American Bandstand on Independence Day:
U.S. Blues

I walked into the Vets Liquor bar about twenty miles outside of DC back in 1976. It was July the 3rd. The Bicentennial was going on in downtown DC and I was heading to the Smoke-In where a few thousand of us Yippies and hippies were going to get together and celebrate our freedom by smoking lots of that devil weed and listening to a variety of rock and roll bands. The government, meanwhile, had its own big show going on with the Beach Boys (or whatever remained of them) and Johnny Cash. And fireworks and military bands.

Anyhow, the jukebox was playing "Okie From Muskogee" and the men and women sitting at the bar were taking the lyrics quite serious as they cast glances my way. My long hair and beard made me look, well, conspicuous. Of course, the upside down US flag sewn on to the back of my jeans (hey it made a great patch) might not have been the friendliest of message to those folks, either. I bought a pack of cigarettes and left without taking my change. Time to get back to friendlier environs.

My thumb went out on Route 1 and I got a ride almost instantly. It was a couple buddies of mine heading out to another suburb which happened to be where I was heading to also. By the end of the day I was in DC smoking some weed with some suburbanites that wasn't doing much and hoping for something better. A group of hippies from West Virginia were sitting about ten feet from me drinking some shine and doing some picking on their guitars and banjo. Nothing too recognizable at first, but they eventually got around to doing a fair version of the Grateful Dead's "Cumberland Blues." I moved into their circle and pulled out a couple joints of some gold-colored weed I'd stashed for a special kind of occasion. The shine made the scene special somehow. Lit one up and passed it on. Can you guys play "US Blues?" They did their best.

But this isn't about smoking weed or even about July 4th. It's about a couple songs from the popular music of the 1960s and afterward that have the United States as their theme. Like the majority of the folks at the smoke-in, most of these types of tunes share a belief that the United States is essentially a good place which has lost its way. Like too many of the folks going to see the government-sponsored fireworks that year (and stay as far away from the Yippees as possible), many other songs of the period are unabashedly nationalistic rallying cries to war and empire. Steppenwolf's "Monster" is perhaps the most pointed of the former from the so-called Sixties, while Lee Greenwood's "God Bless the USA" is certainly one of the most pointed of the latter. Some, like Springsteen's "Born In the USA" are of the former but have often been confused by the apologists for war and empire as a part of the latter's songbook. Then again, some are just celebrations of life in the USA. Chuck Berry's "Livin' In the USA" and James Brown's "Livin' in America." come to mind. On the surface mere apolitical romps, the mere celebration of US life without comment becomes a commentary of its own.

"Monster" by Steppenwolf appears on their 1970 album of the same name. An essentially libertarian anthem, John Kay and his bandmates trace the history of the United States utilizing the previously mentioned template of freedom betrayed. "America," the song asks, "where are you now?" It is about America as a political Frankenstein that has destroyed the nation's original intent. There are no culprits named, but the implicit message is that the politicians and the corporations they serve are the ones who must be removed, since it is their wars we are forced to fight. A present-day expression of this song can arguably be found in James McMurtry's "We Can't Make it Here Anymore"--a song that paints and impressionistic picture of a town and the lives therein destroyed by corporate callousness made possible by politicians without conscience. "Monster" differs in that it expands the scenario into the nation's history. Although this promise is a promise for the colonists and not the natives, the destruction of those peoples and the incorporation of slavery are part of the destruction wrought to the promise.

David Lynn Jones "Living In the Promised Land" sung most famously by Willie Nelson is a song that represents another look at the myth that makes the nation. It is a tale of America from the immigrant's view that promises room for everyone. The United States as the great melting pot. Idealized, for sure, the song does not mention the slaves who came unwillingly bound in ships in conditions worse than sheep and forced to work for the rich white men whose interactions with the native people ended up in the latter's genocide. Yet, it presents a nation formed by immigrants and invites in more while acknowledging there are those already here who have forgotten their own history. When Willie sings "Is there no love anymore/Living in the promised land?" he is reminding the listener that they too come from other lands . Consequently, they should be more than willing to share the hope their ancestors found on America's shores with the newest immigrants. Of course, we know this has rarely been the case.

The Dead's tune "US Blues" is a slightly different take on the US of A. Uncle Sam is, in essence, a con-man. PT Barnum and the pot dealer join the medicine man hucksters wearing Carl Perkins blue suede shoes in a rock and roll traveling show. Unlike the hard-luck working class protagonist of "Born In the USA," the characters of "US Blues" are independent operators whose lives have somehow remained untouched by the miseries of war and the factory. In the concert movie The Grateful Dead Movie, there is an animated sequence that opens the film and features this song. It plays while Uncle Sam is arrested and thrown into jail by a pig-face cop. A cop that looked a lot like some of those on the line that July 4th back in 1976. Cops just waiting for a pot smoking freak to light one up in his face. I recall seeing the Dead in January 1980 at a benefit for Cambodian refugees (that also featured the Beach Boys, among others) where the lyric "Shake the hand that shook the hand of P.T. Barnum and Charlie Chan" was changed to "Shake the hand that shook the hand of P.T. Barnum and the Shah of Iran." This was obviously an ironic reference to the end of that ill-fated relationship in the wake of the Iranian revolution then going on--a revolution Washington is still trying to figure out how to deal with.

I ended up inviting the West Virginia pickers back to my house. On the way home we got pulled over by the county cops. They talked to us for about half an hour, searched the West Virginians' truck and found nothing. While they tossed stuff out of the truck, they half-jokingly asked the guitarist to play a song. He wisely chose Johnny Cash's "Ring of Fire." The lead cop told us how much he liked that song. Then he told us to get the hell home before he decided to look harder. We took his advice. I'm going to be with family up in Maryland this Fourth of July. There will be chicken, burgers, conversation, beer, and music.

Two songs I know I will hear are "Born In the USA" and "God Bless the USA." The irony of the former will be lost on some of my relatives while the complete lack of irony of the latter will be barely tolerated by the rest of us.

Going Where the Water Tastes Like Wine

The only hopes left for those of us who still believed in the countercultural revolution from which our minds had been born were the Grateful Dead, some ultraleft sects, the occasional bluegrass/rock festival, and travel. My friends and I were trying it all with a mixture of drug use thrown in. Our lives were not full. We wanted a life in a culture where everyone else was just looking for a lifestyle.

Over the summer of 1977 some decent weed had made its way to the Baltimore-DC area and weaned us away from the harder stuff. Doreen and I ended up lovers and our group of friends ended up with a couple hundred thousand other lost souls, wanderers, and other societal misfits at a Grateful Dead-headlined concert in New Jersey on Labor Day weekend. That evening, with my mind modified due to the acid I had ingested earlier, I vowed to head west. With the chorus of "California, prophet on the burnin' shore" from the Grateful Dead's song "Estimated Prophet" blasting through the New Jersey night, I knew that by New Year's Eve I would be on that other shore. Three months later, after a few weeks of drudgery making prefab patios at a concrete plant, Doreen (who had been slapping mayo on sandwiches at a deli) and I headed towards the promised land.

It was winter. The Arizona highway stretched out ahead to the western horizon. Finally a ride from the western side of Phoenix to Palm Springs took Doreen and I out of the heat and into what passed for civilization in that part of California. From the back seat I looked around while the driver talked to Doreen in between sips of beer. Coming in from the desert we went into the asphalt manufactured heat and got ever closer to the promised land. After Riverside there was only a few more miles. My mind went wild with hopes and fantasies I might finally realize. California--Los Angeles, San Francisco gold, hippies and Harry Bridges, psychedelia and sexual freedom, movie stars and swimming pools. Berkeley and Oakland and their past and present of Mario Savio and the Black Panthers, People's Park and the Barb, the A's, Giants, Dodgers, Topanga Canyon and Telegraph Avenue.

"Never been to Cal before?" asked the driver.

"No." I replied, my rhapsodic reverie interrupted.

"First time." Said Doreen, pulling long on her beer. I drained what remained in my can – the beer warming quickly in the valley heat blowing through the windows.

"It ain't all it's cracked up to be." Said the driver. "And then again it's more."

The truth of that last sentence was apparent not more than two days after we arrived at our friends' apartment in Huntington Beach. All too soon I remembered that California was also the home of Richard Nixon and Ronnie Reagan. Everything I wanted to escape from in Maryland – the dying counterculture, the pursuit of the dollar, the endless crackerbox suburbias – were all there in California with minimal variations. After a halfhearted attempt to find work in Orange County and a few days of mind expansion with our friends, Doreen and I stuck our thumbs out once again and headed north to the Bay Area.

By evening we were at the foot of University Avenue in Berkeley. Still feeling rich despite our dwindling cash, we rented a room for the night in a cheap motel, bought some beer and relaxed. The next morning we headed towards Telegraph Avenue for breakfast and whatever else awaited us. By that evening we had seen some of the sights and decided that this was the part of California we had in mind when we left the opposite coast.

San Francisco Bay Blues

Doreen and I stumbled out of the Earth People's Park house in Berkeley still hazy from the previous night's mescaline. Rube was sitting on the porch, smoking a cigarette. It was our third night in town and the second place we'd crashed at. This was a house in west Berkeley that had some connection with the chunk of free land in northeastern Vermont known as Earth People's Park. This land was purchased by Wavy Gravy and several other people in the early Seventies and had been a place where folks willing to build their own shelters and live with others in a communal situation could live for free. The payments were rustled up each year through contributions from rock groups and various individuals who shared the ideals of the original purchasers. Wavy used to say that the only reason anybody's name was on the lease was because those who bought and sold property could not conceive of nobody (or everybody) owning a piece of land. That land is no longer free – it's a national reserve of some kind – due to some bikers who used it for drug manufacture and were consequently busted. The federal government than used its forfeiture and seizure laws to steal the land back. However, thanks to an effort spearheaded by Wavy and activist-cinematographer Roz Payne a compromise agreement was reached whereby the land became a nature conservancy. The Berkeley house also had some connection with the San Francisco White Panthers and served as the distribution point for the Panther organized anti-profit food cooperative. The Panthers themselves were a group of counterculture revolutionaries with origins in the Detroit – Ann Arbor area. One of the Detroit's group's founders, John Sinclair, was sentenced to ten years in jail for giving two joints to a narc back in 1969. He later became the focus of a series of concerts organized by yippie Jerry Rubin, Yoko Ono and John Lennon specifically to get him released from jail. The San Francisco group was nominally led a by a guy named Tom and had been squatting a house in the Haight district for years. Occasionally the police would raid the place under some pretext and find a runaway or a firearm. For the most part, however, the neighbors appreciated the collective's presence over that of the police.

Rube latched on to Doreen right away. Not in an annoying or lecherous way but like she was some long lost sister. He took us to the Berkeley Food Project free meal that night and introduced us to a couple decent bars where the beer was cheap and the company entertaining. Within a week or two, he'd turned us on to most of his friends and a couple connections. Even after Doreen and I went our separate ways romantically speaking, he remained friends with us both.

If life is a poker game, Rube was one of those p1ayers who was never dealt an exceptionally good hand but played well with what he had. A bluff here and the right bet there, if you know what I mean. He was arrested on his 17th birthday for smoking pot in some small town outside Albany, New York. The judge, in all his benevolence, gave him the choice of four years in juvenile or two in Vietnam with the Marines. Rube chose Vietnam.

That was the summer of 1967. After an accelerated six weeks of boot camp he found himself in the jungle forward of Danang. His was a standard story. Fire, heat, blood, death. And dope. Rube would laugh every time he lit up a big pipeload of the red Vietnamese pot. Some sentence, he'd grin. Busted for pot in the States and being paid to smoke it in Vietnam. It wasn't until he got to Saigon for a little "r and r" that he tried heroin and fell in love. Eighteen months and a hell of a habit later, his tour was over. What else could he do? He pulled an ace from the pile and requested another year in Nam. The killing machine was chewing up bodies at an increased rate and loved volunteers. He got his extension. By the time his second tour was up, Rube was committed to a life with heroin. The Marines let him go in San Diego and Rube headed to the Bay area. After six months in the Haight, he headed to New York and the Village. He found a job at a rock club where he sold dope on the side to keep his supply steady.

After the club folded in 1971, Rube hopped trains back to California. He ended up in the Santa Barbara switching yards. While buying breakfast one morning he ran into some folks who would become his family. Camping on the beach and smoking a lot of weed, the endless summer really was. When the rains came, they pooled their cash and headed up to Berkeley. After trying their luck on Telegraph Ave. for a few months, his friends went back to Santa Barbara and Rube split for Alaska with a pouch full of acid. Once in Fairbanks he hooked up with a buddy from Vietnam and sold it all. Then he headed into Denali forest for a few weeks. When the nights grew cold, Rube bought a ticket for California, stuck around for a couple of months and then headed to Oaxaca. By the time Doreen and I met him, Rube had been following the same routine for a half dozen years. He had tried to live the so-called straight life while in a love with a woman who grew tired of the nomadic life, but the nine to five routine just didn't sit with his nature.

Loren was another man who had been drafted into the service against his will. When he got his orders to go to Vietnam he took a truck from the motor pool where he worked and ran it through several gates and a couple of parked cars in the Officer's Club parking lot at the base he was stationed. He did six months in the stockade and was thrown out of the Army. He celebrated by going to a rock festival and ended up in Berkeley where he ran into Rube. His father didn't speak to him for years, but it was worth it to Loren just to have avoided the war.

After moving in and out of a variety of cheap hotels and hostels, we finally ended up in a house located off of Foothill Avenue in East Oakland. The neighborhood was ethnically and culturally mixed although primarily black. A few years before we moved in, it had been a stronghold of the Black Panther Party. In fact,

Bobby Hutton Park--a park renamed in honor of the young Panther slain by Oakland police on April 6, 1968--was only four blocks from our house. Although we were glad just to have a guaranteed roof over our heads, the building was actually rather squalid. The house was an old Victorian in need of drastic repair. Some young guy owned it and refused to fix the wiring or the bathrooms. One of our housemates - an adjunct professor at a couple different community colleges in the east bay and official member of the Communist Party-USA--had minimal plumbing skills and that kept the shit going down. As for the neighborhood, junkies stood on the corner and four liquor stores within two blocks took food stamps in violation of the federal laws governing such things. The other housemate was a Vietnam vet who stood six feet four and practiced taekwon do all day long but was afraid to walk to the liquor store a block away. I always thought it was some vestigial racism left over from his youth in St. Louis. The first week there we got ripped off but the thieves didn't find much. Just a jar of change and a leather jacket.

70

Doreen and I continued looking for work and meeting folks. We also went to our share of concerts and demonstrations. One of the demonstrations we went to that May was opposing the presence of the Nazis on the other side of the Berkeley Hills. Now, this part of the Bay Area is very different from San Francisco, Berkeley, and Oakland. It's a land covered with postwar subdivisions, and a predominantly right wing political climate—much like those California counties south of Los Angeles. It was a perfect spot for a demonstration by the American Nazi party.

The whole affair was to take place on a baseball field located in a city park. As we approached the site on foot (after taking the subway to the area), we were stopped by several fully armed police who were herding all of the anti-Nazi demonstrators through a metal detector and choosing certain of us for a more thorough pat-down search. Most of the anti-fascists were either Jewish, pacifists, black, Latino, communist or some combination thereof. Any signs we carried were taken from us, as were pocketknives. Once released from the police, we headed down the path which, with police lining both sides, took on the appearance of a gauntlet. Two more metal detectors later, we made it to the baseball field. The field itself was surrounded by a fifteen foot high temporary chain link fence. As the field filled up with demonstrators, we spent the time chanting and talking among ourselves. The Nazis were scheduled to appear around 1:15 PM.

At approximately 1:00 PM, the police sealed of the entrance to our so-called rally site, which by now was eerily reminiscent of pens used to hold anti-government types in Chile after the coup by Pinochet and the CIA. Once we were sealed in, several dozen more fully armed police marched down the road in formation and proceeded to completely surround the fenced in baseball field. Some of the anti-fascists continued to shout slogans and throw dirt at the police while others of us talked with the officers in an attempt to convince them that protecting Nazis was not in their best interest—especially if they were black or Jewish. Of course, the police officers did not speak. Finally, around 1:30, seven squad cars drove up to the site, their sirens wailing. The police, who were in the front seats of the cars, got out, opened the rear doors and escorted ten men dressed in brown Nazi uniforms to the bleachers behind the backstop. As their leader harangued us, the rest stood at attention while 500 police protected them from our pent-up wrath. Once the speech was over, the Nazis were hustled back into the police cars and driven away. The rest of us were left to make our way back to more tolerant places via the BART train or the highway.

Out of the Haze... Into the Darkness--Recalling 1979

I found myself in San Diego, CA. when 1979 began. Our traveling group of friends had left the environs of Santa Cruz a few months previous because we had been told that San Diego had lots of work. Once we got there, of course, we decided that the only work we really wanted was that of the temporary variety. Fortunately there was enough of that so if we wanted to work we could. My jobs included two weeks at the Buck Knife factory and a month at the Naval Air Station on Coronado Island helping build a computerized mechanism that retrieved parts for fighter planes.. Despite its beaches and the city's hip enclave of Ocean Beach, San Diego turned out to be a town of sailors, conservative old people, and a police force full of klansmen. It was not the place for folks like us. Of course, none of us knew this when we arrived except for R, who had spent some time there when he was in the Navy during the war. This time, R was there less than a week before he landed in jail for an open container. At the time, you could drink outside anywhere outside of downtown. R was holding an open can of beer one block inside of the legal definition of downtown the first time he was busted. After that first arrest, the cops busted and beat him nearly every weekend.

We had closed out 1978 with a Grateful Dead show in San Diego's Golden Hall. The music on the radio left a bit to be desired during this period of rock and roll and I could only listen to so much punk before I stopped hearing it. Nonetheless, I enjoyed the Dead Kennedys wildly anarchistic shows at San Francisco's Mabuhay Gardens and saw the Clash play at a financially disastrous music fest in Monterey in summer 1978. Without a doubt, it was their set along with that of Peter Tosh's that were the highlights of that weekend.

In February, Jimmy Carter brought US forces home from Nicaragua and broke off negotiations with the dictator Somoza. The Shah of Iran was trying to find a place to hide his family after being forced to leave Iran in mid-January. His money had already found a place to hide. Elvis Costello played a rapid-fire forty-five minute set in San Diego's Fox Theatre. They were forty-five of the best musical minutes I ever spent. They played their entire first album and a rock and roll standard or two barely stopping in between songs. The only complaint is I wanted more, but I don't know if Elvis and the Attractions had any more to give.

Rhodesia continued its war against its black inhabitants, despite the growing desire of whites to negotiate a better ending than the one they feared. Afghanistan's left-leaning government was under fire from mujahedin who were being armed by Washington and Saudi Arabia. This decision would come back to haunt Washington in the years to come.

In early March, after winning a rent strike we had organized, most of us left separately for the East Coast where we met up at the Union Grove Fiddlers Convention in North Carolina. As for that rent strike, the moment I relished the most was when a local television news crew came to the building, interviewed a few of the tenants and then turned to ask the landlord some questions. He was a young dapper kind of guy who lived in La Jolla—a rich folks' paradise in the northern part of San Diego county. The first question he was asked was whether our charges of unhealthy and unsafe living conditions was true. This was after the television crew had filmed the water coming through the ceilings and buckets half-filled with rain water in over a dozen different apartments. His answer was that he would never live in a place like this. Even the newscaster on the six-o'clock news looked a little incredulous after that piece was broadcast. Like I said, we won the rent strike. The buildings were re-roofed and we got three months of free rent.

Sometime while we were enroute to the eastern seaboard, the nuclear power plant known as Three Mile Island suffered a partial core meltdown. The stories from the Nuclear Regulatory Commission and the plant's owners exposed their ignorance (and their assumption of our ignorance as well) in the face of impending disaster.   A few days after the fiddlers' convention, the bunch of us went to a Dead show in Baltimore and--a couple days after that--to a huge antinuclear rally in DC. The Dead performed quite well like they did most of the time in those days. The rally was a bit lukewarm in its politics, but the performance by Bonnie Raitt made it worthwhile. Not long afterward, we packed up a friend's VW bus and headed west. The route back to the Golden State this time around was through Pennsylvania, Ohio, Indiana, Illinois, Wisconsin, Minnesota, South Dakota and the Badlands. From there we headed into Utah and across Nevada. By the time we reached Winnemucca, NV. we could almost smell the Pacific and hear its waves calling us to what we regarded as home.

We arrived in Berkeley the day after the riots in San Francisco following the verdict for the ex-cop who killed Harvey Milk and Mayor Moscone. The six of us spent a month or so looking for a place to live. Most landlords rejected any thought of renting to us as soon as they saw our scruffy lot. Eventually, we did find a place. After listening to the landlord, who happened to be the second largest slumlord in the Eastbay, tell us how hard it was to be rich, we got the keys and moved in. Six of us in three bedrooms. We weren't a collective so much as we were a collection of people. We celebrated our new abode with a case or two of malt liquor and a gallon of wine. Bob Dylan's live album from Budokan was the newest album on our playlist. Jimmy Carter made a speech about a national malaise related to Washington's defeat in Vietnam and the corruption and fascist tendencies that had been exposed by the Watergate bust and investigation.. The Sandinistas were our latest heroes as they fought their way towards an eventual victory in Nicaragua. Nicaragua's malaise was being wiped away by revolution.

Sure enough, a couple months later Somoza fled Nicaragua and the Sandinistas were the new government in that country. From all appearances, it seemed that the Nicaraguan people were for the most part happy with the change. Unfortunately, the next president of the United States would not share their enthusiasm. In Afghanistan, the US stepped up its support of a predominantly Islamist insurgency. On November 4th, Iranian students occupied the US Embassy in Tehran, beginning a countdown on evening newscasts in the US that would end only when the hostages were released immediately after Ronald Reagan assumed the presidency in January 1981. The timing of the release of the hostages would eventually be shown to have been arranged by future Reagan officials who promised to work with the rightist elements of the Islamic revolutionary regime and re-arm part of its arsenal by transferring weapons through Israel.

As the year got closer to its end, Jimmy Carter presented the Carter Doctrine to the world. In essence, this doctrine re-emphasized that Washington would do whatever it took to protect so-called vital resources, especially those of the fossil fuel variety. Consequently, this meant Washington would be increasing its military presence in the Middle East and Persian Gulf regions.

Sure enough, within days the Carter administration dispatched the carrier U.S.S. Kitty Hawk and a battle group from the Philippines to the Persian Gulf. Moscow responded in its own way by dispatching Soviet troops to Afghanistan to defend its client government in Kabul. The Cold War was heating up again.

A few days before Christmas, while the sounds of Pink Floyd's The Wall reverberated in our apartment on Berkeley's Dwight Way from the building next door a friend walked in the door with a double album from the Clash titled London Calling. This album was not only the best punk album of the year. It was the best album, period. From the first cut called "London Calling" to the final cut "Train In Vain," this work had everything a rock album could hope to contain. Rebellion, reggae, and straight-out rock and roll. Armageddon, the street, and the essence of love. When our friends who didn't really like punk took a listen to this album, it changed their minds. Meanwhile, the hostages in Iran were still hostages and the wars of Afghanistan were beginning in earnest.

On a personal level, day to day existence during this period was pretty straightforward. No one was chasing the dollar or what passed for comfort in modern

America. We had a car that ran most of the time, a roof over our heads, enough money for beer and pot and the occasional concert and record album. Our clothes were from the free box or second-hand stores. We ate lots of rice, beans and potatoes. Sometimes one of the permanent guests sleeping on our floor would buy us all a meal or some liquor as a form of payment for a place out of the weather. It wasn't expected but it certainly was appreciated. We managed to come up with rent every month and kept the power on.

The 1980s were just around the corner. The beginning of the right wing counterrevolution was at hand. We were not ready for the darkness ahead.

The Lost Art of Hitchhiking

Hitchhiking used to be my carrier of choice. It was cheap and no more dangerous than any other form of transport. Then something changed. Americans grew more isolated from each other and hitchhikers became synonymous with criminals, even though they were more likely to become the victim of a crime. Tom Robbins' big-thumbed heroine Sissy Hankshaw not withstanding, in middle America's mind giving someone a ride became tantamount to committing suicide. Nowadays, it's a rare sight to see a thumb of any size asking for a ride on America's highway.

So, how can I bring it alive for someone who has never been out there along the side of the road thumb up and hoping? You feel like Jack Kerouac. Living that line from the Woody Guthrie song that goes "As I walked down that ribbon of highway, I saw below me that endless valley...."

You notice the desolation of the prairie road which just goes on and on into the horizon. You head toward the mountains that look so close but take a good day's ride to reach. At dusk, you hear sound of the lonesome whippoorwill. In midday, the relentless heat of the southwestern desert beats on your shoulders and on the eastern highways; the suffocating humidity of the east coast's summer sends beads of sweat down the bridge of your nose.

The big eighteen-wheelers that zoom by nearly pulling you into their wake. A rainstorm that comes out of nowhere when there's no shelter in sight and proceeds to split the sky in a light show from the gods that takes your breath away just before you reach the overpass.

Getting picked up by a biker driving a van with his disassembled Harley in the back. He took me home and then out drinking in a bar outside Toledo, Ohio where I scored umpteen million points on the pinball machine while his buddies drove their Harleys through the place. The farmer who didn't pick me up and looked straight ahead as if I wasn't there. Then there was the uptight family man with the "I Love Jesus" bumperstickers who gave me the finger as I stood on a ramp near Chicago's stockyards. Or the teenage boys driving daddy's car that drove by once and threw a full can of beer at my head. Then, on their second time around, they stopped and urged me to climb in. A nurse who took me home and slept with me that night and the guy with the poodle who tried to. Once, sleeping by the side of the road near

Oklahoma City I awoke in the morning to find an Apache girl at my side. Only trying to keep warm, she said, and keep the snakes away.

Two junkies who picked me up near Pueblo, Colorado and were heading to Midland, Texas, man, to score a quarter ounce of Mexican mud heroin. Two pretty teenage girls on their way to Milwaukee from Chicago who wanted me to buy beer for them. We drank until all three of us were so drunk we couldn't drive. The car of Jesus freaks in Tennessee who slowed down like they were going to give me a ride then, after running a quarter mile to their car, they gave me some tracts and pulled away.

One June day in the late 1970s Doreen, Bonita, and I headed up to Eugene, Oregon from Berkeley with our sleeping bags, 75 dollars, a good-sized stash, and our backpacks for a rock festival. We arrived at the end of University Avenue in Berkeley right before the I-80 bridge at 8:30 in the morning and claimed our spot amongst the dozen or so hitchhikers already there. We didn't get on the road until noon. But then we rolled straight on through to just south of Sacramento. The exit ramp we stood on there was one of those that seemed to be built for the private use of some rancher.

No town could be seen in any direction on a horizon flatter than a tabletop and no cars traveled on the one road headed off to the east.

The three of us had pretty much given up hope on getting any further that day and looked around half-assed for a suitable spot to sleep. The closest trees were a couple miles away. It was a pretty hot day so we decided to stay near the road at least until the day cooled. Then, if we were still there, head over to the trees. Not more than twenty minutes after that decision, an RV pulled over and the driver told us to hop in back. After getting back on the road we headed towards the coast. The driver didn't like taking his vehicle on the desert--like path I-5 carved like a ditch through central California. When we turned north onto Highway 1, I fired up a joint and settled back for a long, winding journey. Bonita and Doreen did likewise.

The combination of the weed and the road soon put me to sleep. The next thing I remember was crossing into Oregon with two more passengers in the truck. Bonita and Doreen were now up front in the cab while I shared the back with a big red-haired guy who said he was AWOL from the Navy and his buddy, a thin bearded guy I recognized from the streets of Santa Cruz.

The first thing I was asked once the two realized I was awake was which one of the two babes was my old lady. I began to say that neither one was old anything, but all those two heard was the neither of them part. I sensed there was going to be a problem. Bonita and Doreen, meanwhile, had discovered that the driver was a jewel thief who traveled around the country burglarizing, recutting, and fencing jewels. However, other than his choice of professions, he was very careful to stay within the law. After all, if he was stopped by the cops for anything he was as good as gone, being wanted in several states.

About an hour south of Eugene, my fellow RV occupants broke out a gallon of port wine and began drinking. I noticed the driver looking nervously at them in his rearview mirror. He opened the little window between the cab and the passenger part of the vehicle just to assert his presence, I think. He didn't say anything, though, until they started talking trash to the two women. After five or so minutes of listening to their remarks, the driver stopped his truck on the shoulder and asked Red and Santa Cruz to get out. They told him to fuck off and pulled long from their bottle. The driver got out, grabbed Red's pack and tossed it on the ground.

I knew that was a bad move and prepared myself for the worst. Santa Cruz reached into his boot and pulled out a knife. Red was out of the RV and going to retrieve his pack. I picked up the empty wine bottle he'd left behind, ready to use it as a weapon if necessary. Santa Cruz hopped out of the truck and threatened the driver with his knife. I threw Santa Cruz's pack out the rear and, in the confusion, Red and his buddy got left behind and the rest of us finished the ride to Eugene.

Long Live People's Park! Showdown in the Counterculture Corral

In April of 1969, an eclectic bunch of people in Berkeley, California reclaimed a piece of land owned by the University of California, dug up the asphalt parking lot there, tilled the soil, planted trees and plants, put in a swing set and benches and turned it into a park. Black Panthers, street people, elderly women and men, students, children and dogs all joined in to make the park a piece of liberated territory. It became know as People's Park.

The University, with the urging of then governor Ronnie Reagan, decided to end this endeavor in neighborhood land reclamation. Reagan and the rest of the university's regents were already ticked off about the Third World Strike that had effectively shut down the Berkeley campus for much of the spring semester. The creation of the park was the last straw. Reagan and the university administration decided to do something. On May 15, 1969 University police took back the park in a pre-dawn raid. They arrested the street people who were sleeping there and sealed off an eight-block area around the park. A construction crew came in and begin to fence off the park's perimeter. At noon, a rally of over

6000 people was held in Sproul Plaza protesting the police occupation of the park. The rally ended with a march to the park. All hell broke loose once the protesters met up with police from all over the East Bay. Police fired shotguns, killing James Rector and wounding over 100 others. All public assembly was banned and the National Guard was activated. For the next two weeks, a state of insurrection existed in Berkeley. The park remained fenced off. In the years immediately following, the fence around the park became a ready target whenever Berkeley erupted into protest. After a particularly raucous protest in 1972 after Nixon mined the harbor of Haiphong, Vietnam, the fence was torn down for the last time and the city of Berkeley leased the land for a nominal sum and let it be administered by a council of citizens and park habitués-the People's Park Council. Since that time, the university has attempted to reclaim the park land a half-dozen times or so, only to be met with protest and ultimately backing down.

The park recently celebrated its 34th year as liberated territory. It has not been without its problems, but it has always remained as a symbol and a reality. What follows is a remembrance of a 1979 attack on the park's existence by the University-an attack that was resisted by community action and solidarity.

Another showdown. For those who were around in 1969 or 1972, it was an eerie deja vu. Some of the same cops and some of the same fighters in the battle for People's Park were facing off again. The park was a piece of land that the University of California had been attempting to develop since the late Sixties and had been rebuffed by determined community resistance each time. The veterans on both sides were all a little grayer, but the grudges remained. For most of us, though, it was the first major battle. This was a different battle than those daily skirmishes where the cops swaggered through the park spreading their porcine presence. They'd walk over to a group of folks and demand identification, just because they could. If you refused, you went to jail. No questions, just handcuffs. This was counterinsurgency of a certain type.

The University of California had pushed it too far this time. The afternoon before, a couple dozen members of their police force escorted a bulldozer into the park and began removing benches. The morning paper had written about a University administrative plan to start charging for the westend parking lot-the only remaining asphalt in the park. We had heard rumors about this possibility for months yet in the Council's negotiations with the University they insisted the rumors were lies. More bureaucrats speaking with forked tongues. The bulldozer was phase one. One of the park's denizens --a big mean guy named Tommy Trashcan -- walked over to the dozer and pulled out the ignition wires. I never liked the fellow before or after that act, but at that moment he was my hero. The police attempted to arrest him as more cruisers arrived. After a twenty-minute tussle, Trashcan was in the police van. It was immediately surrounded by a couple dozen folks, who sat on the ground around the van. The cop at the wheel revved his engine and charged through the crowd. After that, somebody went to the tool shed in the bushes at the other end of the lot and brought out a couple of pickaxes. We took turns removing the asphalt in the parking lot piece by piece. After giving us a series of unheeded warnings the cops left, bragging to us that they would win and take the park back.

Before dawn the next morning several hundred enraged citizens hung around in the park and the surrounding sidewalks. The University had installed machines overnight that dispensed tickets at the entrances to the parking lot overnight. Some of us who were hanging out passed out leaflets urging drivers to park elsewhere, some drank an early morning beer, and some sharpened sticks for use in the attack they felt sure was coming. In the parking lot across Haste Street were the police. Maybe a hundred cops milled around drinking coffee, putting on their riot gear and talking on their radios. They were preparing for battle as seriously as those looking for one on our side of the street. The adrenalin levels were high all around.

About half an hour before the University had commanded the new pay parking lot to open, a bus from the Hog Farm commune that they called the Asp drove up. While some of the parks swarthier defenders removed the machines demanding parking fees from the earth, the Asp's inhabitants began handing out balloons and tying a string of them around the park. Those of us in the park smiled a little, our tenseness eased a bit by the Hog Farmers' antics. As I watched the officers across the street however, I noticed that their apprehension didn't seem to change. Indeed, their desire to attack only seemed to be enhanced by the Hog Farmers' lightheartedness.

As the defining moment approached, Salty, a member of the park's organizing and maintenance committee, spoke on the phone to the mayor, Communist Party member Gus Newport. The Hog Farmers continued to distribute balloons. Somebody, maybe it was Wavy Gravy, was playing Reveille on a kazoo. While the Farmers were finding plenty of takers among the citizens in the park and those who came to park, they couldn't even pay one of the cops to take one. Just as the riot squad moved into their attack formation and pulled down the clear plastic visors on their helmets, the mayor drove up. He got out of his car and waved good morning to the park's defenders. Then he told the police to leave. Since he was the city cops' boss they did so, cursing, one can be sure, the commie son of a bitch all the way back to their cars. This left a much-reduced force of University police who could do little but observe. Which they did for six weeks.

During those six weeks the parking lot was removed piece by piece and the beginnings of a garden were put in place. The occupation of the park enjoyed tremendous support for the first month. The first couple weeks' worth of evenings, in fact, turned into big picnics with folks from all around the Bay Area bringing food, beer, pot and music makers. Merriment reigned those nights as people met new friends and hung out with old ones. Professionals with loosened ties on their way home from work joined together with hardened park habitués, musicians, college students and brothers from the streets of Oakland and West Berkeley and began to plant a garden where the parking lot had stood. Local businesses brought donations of plants and building supplies. As time went on, though, the picnics got smaller, and eventually the only people who remained were those who had nowhere else to go. This was mostly a collection of street people, petty criminals who made their living from selling bogus dope to tourists, and hard-core gypsies. Two days after Thanksgiving the cops moved in and sent everyone on their way.

The anger remained, however, as did the garden planted in that former parking lot. Over the next few months a stage was built in the park and those of us who still believed in the park's essential difference from the rest of America's "private property" and weren't too disillusioned for whatever reason, continued a public campaign in the park's behalf. Concerts were planned, agreements with the university penned, and gardens maintained.

We also started a newspaper called, simply, The People's Park Press, which served the dual purpose of keeping the larger community informed and the street community involved in its own destiny. Articles ran the gamut from street gossip to analysis of various local and international political realities and were written by park regulars. Everything seemed to be moving forward. The spring began with a couple concerts that came off quite well. Robert Hunter of the Grateful Dead played a May gig there, as did a band formed by a couple former members of Creedence Clearwater Revival. Despite some rather disconcerting public sex in one corner of the park, things went smoothly. Not Disney World, but not bad for a bunch of freaks.

It must have been the third or fourth concert of the year when the cops decided to end the fun. A hardcore punk band from across the bay had just begun their second song after a rousing speech calling for dope legalization by a peoples' lawyer named Joe when the plug was pulled. Literally. A sympathetic businessperson on Telegraph Avenue allowed bands to plug in to his power source via a couple of very long extension cords and the police just yanked them. After they drove away from the scene, the cords were plugged back in and some of the more menacing concertgoers stationed themselves along the wires to protect them from the cops. The officers then threatened the shop owner with a variety of charges if he didn't unplug the band. To his credit he didn't. Five minutes later, ten policemen pushed their way past the shop owner to the back of his store, unplugged the cords and cut off the plugs, rendering the cords useless.

The band hurriedly packed up its equipment while those of us in the park grumbled and lit up the joints distributed during Joe's legalization talk. After most of the band's equipment was loaded into their van, Joe took the stage. Asking people not to leave, he urged us all to take the party to the streets. As he shouted, fifty or so people wandered a half block down Haste Street to where it intersected Telegraph. Some of us began re-directing traffic while others sat down in the intersection, nervously waiting for whatever came next. Meanwhile, teenagers who came in every weekend from surrounding towns left their aimless wandering up and down the Avenue and joined the swelling crowd in the street. Jackson started playing his guitar and money was collected for beer and weed. The cops were ignored as they tried to clear the streets.

Meanwhile, in the park a half-dozen officers were trying to arrest Joe and a couple of his friends. He managed to slip away from the cops and made it to the party in the street. Excitedly, he told us what was going on. Just as he was finishing, several police vehicles pulled up and emptied themselves of several dozen cops in riot gear. Two of them grabbed Joe and began wrestling him to the ground. All hell broke loose. Bottles and rocks flew, windows were smashed and the police began hitting whomever they could reach. Then just as quickly as it began, the melee ended and the police pulled back. The street party grew and didn't end until evening when police from Berkeley and Oakland formed themselves into a wedge formation and cleared the streets. The next morning the street cleaners were joined by some of the park's early risers as they swept up the trash from the day before.

Goo Goo Ga Joob...Remembering John Lennon

It's easy to remember the date: December 8, 1980. I was sitting at a friend's house in Berkeley listening to music and talking. Another fellow was in the house kitchen talking with his parents who lived in North Carolina. Somewhere in the house a television was broadcasting Monday Night Football. It was just another Monday night when a shriek came first from the kitchen and then from the room with the television. The nature of the shriek caused the conversation I was having to stop as we went to investigate.

"John Lennon is dead! Someone fuckin' murdered him!"

The house was suddenly silent. Not knowing what else to do, I went to the record collection and found the house's copy of John's first solo album, Plastic Ono Band, and put "Working Class Hero" on the turntable. We listened to that song and then I headed out the door, wondering what was happening at my place of residence. When I arrived there, at least a dozen friends were sitting in the common room listening to Beatles records and drinking beer and wine. A wake was in progress. It continued for days in Berkeley and around

98

the world. What follows is a slightly enhanced account of one in Berkeley. Names have been changed to protect the not-so-innocent.

"Sure do wish I'd get a ride." thought Silver Star as she crossed 28th Street where it intersected Telegraph Avenue near downtown Oakland. Nothing but loudmouths driving their road monsters -- the orange glow of the sunset reflecting off the windshields -- and shouting hey baby I'll give you a ride but what'll you give me? Assholes I ain't riding with that's for sure. She reached 41st and went into a liquor store directly across from the Doggie Diner where she bought her third quart of malt liquor for the day. Beatles' music played there, too. The Lebanese guy behind the counter whistled the tune as he rang up her purchase. Everywhere you went since Monday all you heard was Beatles or John Lennon music since that asshole killed John. Everybody seemed kind of estranged from each other and the world, too. More than usual, even. Hopefully, the public wake would clear some of the weirdness from the air. That's why she was going. Even if she had to walk the whole five miles. She slung her leather jacket over her shoulder, tucked the quart bottle under her arm, and continued north on Telegraph.

I stood at the bus stop on San Pablo Avenue, reading a handbill I'd found in the street on the walk from my house closer to the bay.

JOHN LENNON WAKE
Singing and meditation
for our recently murdered brother
1st Unitarian Church
Berkeley, CA.
7:30 PM Thursday
Bring instruments and refreshments

Underneath was a picture of John Lennon. It was the one from the white album, where his hair is pretty long but he doesn't have a beard. I had heard about this thing on Tuesday but this was the first time I'd seen any of the details. I pocketed the leaflet, noticed the bus was one stop away, and dug in my pocket for the fare. It stopped in front of me and I boarded the bus and sat down. Silently singing the words to "Nowhere Man", I looked blankly out the window at the traffic and other human activity on the street. By the time I got to the second chorus, it was time to disembark. I pulled the bell cord, and when the bus stopped, left through the rear door, walked to the corner of the block and turned left, the setting sun at my back.

Hurrying past the first two apartment buildings on Channing Way, I turned left into the third driveway, walked up the front steps of the house and knocked. Somebody inside opened the door a crack, saw that it was me, and let me in.

"Hi, Z," I said. "What's up?"

"Hey, Ron," said Z, his huge beard sudsy from drinking beer. "How ya' doin'? Got any smoke? We're just sitting around watching the tube."

"Oh, yeah?" I closed the door behind him and pulled a cigarette-sized joint from my jacket pocket. "What's on?"

"Some special on John Lennon." replied Z, taking the joint and lighting it with a cigarette. "See, there's some footage from that Live/Peace in Toronto concert. In fact, there's ol' what's his name on lead."

"Eric Clapton." I responded.

"Yeah, right. He sure looks different." agreed Z, handing the joint to some girl sitting behind him on the floor.

"Shit, they all do. Man, I love Klaus Voorman's bass playing at this show."

Z sat down on the floor and rolled another joint. When he was finished he stuck it between his lips and lit it. After a long draw, he handed it to me, just as I remembered the handbill in my pocket and handed it to Z.

Z read it and looked up. "You goin'?" he asked.

"Yeah."

"Maybe I'll see ya' there."

"All right." I turned towards the door. "Well, I've gotta' go get something to eat somewhere and get to that wake all on the same transfer. Ciao."

"I'll see ya' there," yawned Z.

I found the Unitarian church easily. Once there, I opened the door and heard the piano. Somebody was banging out "Love Me Do" and ten or fifteen people were more or less singing it. They sounded drunk and out of tune. As I entered the meeting room, I was surprised at how few people there were but glad to see plenty of beer and wine. Maybe more people would show up later. Most people didn't like thinking about death anyway.

By the time I finished my first beer the place was filled with people -- mourners, if you will. A couple guitarists and a woman playing flute had joined the guy playing piano. When she played it sounded a little jazzy. Looking around after grabbing another beer from one of the ice and beer filled trashcans in the room, I noticed Z entering through the door. I watched him open a beer and and head towards a circle of people on the floor in the center of the room. There was a lit candle in the middle of the circle and everyone was holding hands. Oh Jesus, another om-ing circle. Z and I were perpetually making fun of this kind of pseudo-spiritual stuff. I chuckled as I watched a grin appear beneath Z's unruly facial hair, rose from my chair and wandered across the room, slipping between and around clusters of people until I stood next to Z.

"Hi, Z. What's up?"

"Hey, Ron. Cheers." said Z, clanging his beer can against mine. "Or don't you say 'cheers' at a wake?"

"No, you just get drunk, I think." I deadpanned, watching the people in the circle. They were moving their joined hands in a series of motions and chanting something I couldn't quite make out. "What are they saying?"

Z swallowed a mouthful of chips and replied, "It sounds like something from the Book of Law or some other Aleister Crowley craziness."

"Oh yeah," I remembered. "I forgot you know that shit. What? Are they trying to bring John back from the dead?"

Those in the circle now let go of each other's hands and formed themselves into a pentagram. Someone blew the flame in the center out and the chanting stopped.

"I don't know," answered Z. "They never will though. I think he likes it there."

"We'll see. Couldn't be much worse." I agreed. "How was the rest of that TV show?"

"You saw the best part. After that, it slipped into typical TV docudrama emptiness. You got any herb? I left mine at home."

I pulled a bag from my pocket and handed it to Z. We both sat down on the floor and Z began to roll.

Maybe that friggin' church is on the next block thought Silver Star. She'd been there before during the day for some women's meeting. Looking behind her fearfully for that white Fairlane and hoping she wouldn't see it, she continued to run blindly towards where she thought the church was. She couldn't believe that after being so careful about her rides she got picked up by those assholes. It must be because she got too drunk and her psychic sense short-circuited. Whatever it was...those assholes holding a knife on her and hitting her with their fists while that fat pig stuck his -- she can't even think about that part 'cause it makes her want to puke. She's gotta' block it out. Or she might kill the next man she sees even though all men aren't pigs it's hard to remember that in times like this. Shit, where is that church? She must have run a mile by now. At least from San Pablo she thought. It seemed like it was just a couple blocks north of University where those assholes pushed her out of the car. Near that ribs place -- only on the other side of the street. It's hard to remember the fuckin' details when all she keeps seeing in her mind is that fat pig's dick and that knife in her face. If they hadn't had that hunting knife she probably would have bit his fuckin' thing off. Just so he could never do to anyone else what he did to her. Hell...she can't remember where they took her or their license number or even their faces just that fuckin' knife and that, that.... Goddam, where is that church?

Wait, looks like there's a lot of cars up ahead -- maybe that's the place. Whatever it was maybe she could find someone to talk to. Someone who could help her calm down at least enough to try and remember. She ran to the outer doors and pulled them open. She heard the Beatles' music. "A Hard Day's Night" in fact, sung by what sounded like a bunch of drunks.

She needed to talk to someone. Someone who could help her -- a woman. But she didn't see any women she knew. There sure were a lot of people, though. Three or four hundred at least. She looked around a bit more slowly now and thought she saw Rollerboy and Z by the coolers of beer. Well, if there wasn't anybody else, they could help her.

"Hey, Ron," asked Z. "Isn't that Silver Star?"

I looked in the direction Z was pointing and saw Silver Star's head above the crowd. She seemed out of it. More than that, she looked like she'd been hurt. Pretty bad. You know. Her hair all tangled. A few cuts. Dazed. Z and I watched her walk across the room. The closer she got, the worse she looked.

"Damn," said Z. "She doesn't look so good."

"Really."

"I mean, she looks like hell." exclaimed Z. "Like she's totally freaked." She was almost next to us now.

"I've been raped, Ron!" screamed Silver Star, crying and trying to talk at the same time. "Some guys picked me up on Telegraph near Alcatraz and took me somewhere and held a knife on me and -- oh, man, it was rude, it --"

"Silver Star," I said, trying to sound calm. The music had stopped completely and everyone in the room was staring at us. "Let's go sit down. Can you do that?"

"Yeah, but raped, Ron. Those pigs. I just can't block it out." She grabbed Z and I as if she were afraid we might leave.

"Don't try to right now, Silver Star." comforted Z. "Let's go sit down somewhere. Maybe smoke some weed."

"That might help," she agreed, her grip on the two of us loosening a bit. We headed to a corner of the room, stopping by one of the trashcans and grabbing three beers on the way.

The piano player began playing again and the singers singing and everyone else went back to what they were doing before, eager to pretend they never heard what Silver Star said. I knew that none of them really wanted to involve themselves in someone else's problems even if it was their problem, too. It was easier to mourn the dead. We walked over to a bench setting against the wall opposite the piano. I helped Silver Star sit down while Z rolled another joint. As he rolled, the pianist and his drunken choir sang the chorus to "Nowhere Man". You know, when John sings that line about just seeing what you want to see, just a bit like you and me?

Cratched Does California

It must have been around 10 in the morning of Christmas 1981 and the beans and rice from last night's meal had long since stopped filling our stomachs. R and I had been on Telegraph since 8:00 or so feeling like Dylan's Mr. Tambourine Man. You know--jingle jangle morning and all that. At least the sun was shining. It was California after all.

As the morning passed, about the only other people we saw on the street were some disgruntled policemen who preferred to be home with their families, a hobo or two, and some people going to the church near the university. Oh yeah, and the Persian guy who had a flower stand in front of Cody's bookstore that was open until 2:00 PM Christmas day for those folks who had forgotten to buy a gift for their lover or their mom or someone else who appreciated flowers. R and I didn't have anyone like that, nor did it seem like there would be anybody like that in our near future.

It was around noon when a couple frat boys drove up Telegraph in their BMW and yelled something at us. I don't know whether it was pleasant or not--after a while you just tune out people who have a history of harassing you and frat boys had that kind of history, as did people driving BMWs.

Anyhow, after that car drove by, we noticed the smell of fresh roasted turkey wafting down the avenue. You know how in the cartoons they show the aroma of good food floating like waves across the screen and into some character's nose? Then the character floats on the fumes towards their source and, just before the dog or cat eats the meat, a human hand appears and takes it away.

Well, that's how it was with us. That turkey aroma was pulling us in like a sugar donut pulls in flies. We were so hungry we followed the aroma up the street to a midscale restaurant where all we could do was stare at the people eating their Christmas dinners. Nice big slabs of turkey, piles of mashed potatoes with gravy, rolls and butter, pies of pumpkin, pies of mincemeat, all the good things in life. And bottles of wine and beer, too. I would do anything to get some of that food, but what I did instead was walk back down the street with R and ingest the fumes.

If we weren't depressed before, we definitely were now. I was ready to go back to the apartment and boil some more beans, if there were any left. R was ready to just give up. We looked at each other and began to walk away from Telegraph Avenue when the Persian guy called Hey! I looked over, wondering if he was yelling at us or someone else. He looked right at me and beckoned me over to his stand. Bring your friend, he said. I grabbed R by the coat and we walked over to his stand, wondering what was up. Maybe he was going to ask us to sweep for him and give us a couple bucks. He reached under where he kept his money box in his cart and pulled out two steaming styrofoam to-go containers.

I don't celebrate your holiday, he said, I am of Islam. But you guys need, what do you say, Christmas cheer. Then he handed us each a hot turkey dinner with a slab of turkey, piles of potatoes and gravy, rolls and butter and a piece of pie. I took the mincemeat and R took the pumpkin. We felt like two twentieth-century Bob Cratcheds in Ronnie Reagan's America.

Remembering Ronnie Rayguns' Morning in America

In 1981, a crazed rich kid shot Ronald Reagan. For many folks in Berkeley it was a dream of revenge come true. After all, it was Reagan who called for a bloodbath in the town after he ordered the National Guard into Berkeley in response to the 1969 Third World Strike at the university and the People's Park insurrection the same year. It was Reagan and his henchmen who had helped imprison, murder and isolate the Black Panthers and the radical left in the Bay Area. It was Reagan who was partially responsible for the rightwing resurgence in America resurgence that has yet to ease it deadly grasp. As the television screen showed the assassination attempt over and over again, we wondered if the old fascist would make it through. Like our buddy Loren said as we watched, it's not that he would wish anyone dead; it's just that he wouldn't shed any tears if Reagan ended up that way--sooner rather than later.

Berkeley was one place in the country that did not rejoice when Reagan won the presidency. In fact, a spontaneous protest of several thousand people erupted. The protest ended with the man being burned in effigy and an occupation of the administration building at the university. My friend R and I were among forty-five people who refused to leave at closing time and were dragged out by the police. The District Attorney did not prosecute any of us. Instead, he brought us each in for a meeting where he tried to convince us that we should work through the system. After all, he told us, he never really effected change until he quit demonstrating in the streets and went back to school to get his law degree. Then he got to tell us hardcore dropouts and radicals to register to vote.

After watching the reruns of the shooting a couple dozen more times, R, Loren and I headed over to Telegraph Avenue to see what was happening. The word of Reagan's bout with death had reached the street rather quickly and people were beginning to party. The scene was (in a muted way) slightly reminiscent of those pictures you may have seen of the liberation of Paris in World War II or the streets of Teheran after the Shah was unseated from power. People were openly sharing their beers and other drinks while the police stood around somewhat nervously, wondering how to react. Some punkers in a hearse drove up the street several times honking their horns and shouting, The King is Dead out the windows of their vehicle. Street veterans of the battles of Berkeley in the Sixties and Seventies drank deeply and smiled. Shop owners who shared our opinions beamed. The party went on until dark. Reagan survived, probably because he would have needed a stake driven through his heart to die.

I had become aware over time of how different our lives and ideas were from mainstream America. After Reagan's election this distance became even greater. Every time I left the Bay Area the Reagan effect was omnipresent. People actually liked the man despite his complete lack of depth or character. Perhaps, now that I think of it, that is why they liked him because he had none of either. The rebirth of anti-Left and ultimately anti-democratic impulses under Reagan were not only tolerated by most US citizens, they were celebrated. Greed and material ownership were heralded as the ultimate realization of the American dream. Freedom was defined solely in terms related to the freedom to manipulate others in the pursuit of profit. If I were more of a religious person, I wouldn't hesitate to say that it was mammon, not God, who ruled America. This, in spite of the commonly held belief that America's wealth was somehow related to Gods beneficence--a belief perpetrated by the moralistic hypocrites who had helped finance Mr. Reagan's election (and who peopled his administration).

Another development that was part and parcel of Ronnie Reagan's "morning in America" was the increasingly desperate scene on the streets. A life that seemed to be a matter of choice for a good number of my fellows when I first hit the street had become a struggle for those of us who remained and those who arrived daily, thanks to the growing unemployment. We were living an American hallucination, although how much of it was someone else's hallucination and how much of it the result of our own psychedelic-fueled vision will never be determined. Nonetheless, our dream was looking more and more like a nightmare. Somewhere in the country there was an abundance of wealth, but it surely wasn't on Telegraph Avenue, the transient communities of the nation, its inner city ghettos, prisons, or the road and train yards. In these places where the very poor gathered, people fought each other over six packs of beer and packages of cigarettes while in the opposite economic sphere, the battles were (like always) over money and politics.

That hallucination has become the everyday reality some twenty years later. Unemployment continues to rise and most of those folks who were on the outside then do not even register in the statistics anymore. The powers of the police, who had too much power, then, are greater than even the most paranoid of us could have envisioned. The Islamic fundamentalist guerrillas that he funded to fight the Soviets have come back to pay their respects. Ronald Reagan's heir apparent--George Bush--has not only done the old guy one better by stealing the White House, he has much of Reagan's court in the palace with him. It is a court that believes it has no obligation to the rest of the world, much less this nation. Morning in America? Those guys must have stolen some of those night-vision goggles that the military uses, because it's been dark around these parts for a while.

Christmas in Prison

It was December again, maybe a week before Christmas. Southwester and I were selling propeller baseball hats. Rainbow hued. The game within the game. Keeps the sun out of eyes and puts your head above the clouds.   There were lots of buyers that day on Telegraph Avenue. With only four shopping days until Christmas, suburbanites were out in force and spending their cash as they enjoyed the freak show that was Telegraph Avenue. Southwester was going full blast with his spiel. He was in top form. Like that night I first met him a couple years earlier in San Francisco hustling "Nobody for President" stickers to a Grateful Dead crowd. Vote for Nobody. Nobody will solve the world's problems. Nobody will legalize pot. Nobody loves you when you're down and out. And so on.

This day Southwester wore his hat low over his right eye like he'd done since his teenage days as a pachuco in Oxnard. Oxnard where he spent his first sixteen years helping his family scrape out an existence. His dad worked for the railroad sometimes and his mom and the kids picked fruit when it was fruit picking time   His youthful recreation was drinking ripple, smoking cheap Mexican weed, a little bit of gang fighting, and Chicana girls. After high school , which he left early by mutual arrangement, he headed to New York City.

One afternoon in Sheep's Meadow at a rock concert he caught the eye of a woman who wrote for *Downbeat*. Tripping on good acid, he followed her home to her loft in the East Village. They fell in love and their loft became a spot of underground renown. Southwester ran with the counterculture revolutionaries the Up Against the Wall Motherfuckers raising a little bit of political hell. Kesey and his pranksters stopped at the loft and, somewhere between the first bus trip and Woodstock, the two climbed on the bus. He ended up with the Hog Farm. This was a group that got its start after Kesey went to Mexico to escape some jail time over a pot bust. Despite Kesey's absence, the Pranksters continued doing the acid tests. After a test in Watts, some of the Pranksters headed to Mexico to meet up with him. The rest of them stayed behind and eventually got a job caretaking a movie producer's hog farm in the hills west of Los Angeles. Hence the name Hog Farm. This crew became quite well known in the counterculture, especially after taking a job as food distributors and peace force for the Woodstock festival in 1969. After years of wandering the country in their caravan of buses they ended up in Berkeley.

It was years later now. Southwester's hair was gray where he still had any. The kids he'd joined up with for the trip had kids of their own. He and I stood on the corner of Telegraph and Haste Street, sharing a cigarette and talking up the propeller caps when three cop cars pulled up, their lights aglow. Southwester began gathering up his wares figuring they were about to cite him for not having a current vendor's license. I stood quietly, running down an inventory of my pockets trying to recall if they were holding anything illegal.

The next thing I knew I was up against the wall being searched. Southwester was in one cop's face asking what the story was. They ignored him so he started talking louder. Three more cruisers pulled up as a crowd gathered. I considered struggling, but changed my mind as I saw six cops get out of the three recent vehicular additions to their forces. Southwester backed off a bit and the cops started pushing people back with their sticks. Our friend Creamcheese pushed a cop out of the way and he whacked her once with his club. I was told there was a warrant out for my arrest for being present during a marijuana sale to an undercover cop. Merry Christmas, I thought.

Standing Up to El Diablo--The 1981 Blockade of the Diablo Canyon Nuclear Power Plant

September 14, 1981. I had just been released from the Berkeley jail after being arrested in front of a Grateful Dead concert the day before. Returning to the place I shared with a group of friends, I got ready to head off to San Luis Obispo where an attempted occupation and blockade of the Diablo nuclear power plant was underway.

This protest was organized by the Abalone Alliance-a coalition of hardcore pacifists, left Democrats and non-affiliated left liberals who seemed to believe that if they flew the US flag and convinced enough people to ask politely without yelling at the cops or the officials of the utility company, the plant would never go online. Their ploy did not work. Nonetheless, I wanted to take part in their attempt. After meeting up with my friend Joe at the Earth People's Park house in West Berkeley, he and I headed out to the foot of University Avenue to hitch down Route 101 to the protest. Eight hours later we were in a camp set up on a few acres of land that a sympathetic farmer had provided. Our friends and fellow affinity group members-Southwester and Ross-were already there.

The camp itself was a model of alternative forms of energy. The showers were constructed from sanitized fifty gallon drums painted a flat back to absorb and store heat, which in turn heated the water. These drums were set on wooden racks about nine feet high. Pieces of recycled hose were attached with spigots which, when opened, allowed the water to flow. Several ovens powered by wooden and solar heat had been built from rocks and recycled aluminum and semi-private outhouses were also provided. At the end of each day, there would be a meeting of spokespeople from each of the affinity groups in the camp. Most of these meetings had to do with logistics and strategy around the blockade. However, one evening it seemed like all we talked about was the US flag that flew in the center of the camp. Some of the more radical campers had tried to remove it earlier and were met with considerable resistance by the flag's supporters. As it turned out, most of those who had attempted to pull down the flag were members of the Revolutionary Communist Youth Brigade (RCYB)-the RCP's youth wing. The next thing I knew, the argument was no longer about the flag but about whether or not communists should be allowed to participate in the plant blockade. This is when

Southwester and I jumped into the argument. We weren't RCP members, but we weren't Democrats or pacifists, either. Plus, we didn't care much for flags, black, red or red, white and blue. It looked like the flag argument was going to split the camp in two when someone proposed a compromise: fly the flag but fly it upside down. This compromise worked and the camp held together.

To me the most telling part of the whole Diablo Canyon action occurred on the morning our network of affinity groups was set to block the plant and prevent workers and police from gaining entrance. Although I had qualms about intervening in the construction workers' livelihood, those concerns were dropped when one of their union representatives told us that the construction workers were paid whether they made it into the plant site or not. That concern resolved, our group of six, which included three of my buddies from the streets of Berkeley--Joe, Southwester, and Ross-- decided that we should block the road a mile or so away from the plant, since this was not an area where demonstrators were officially allowed according to an agreement reached between the protest organizers and the police. Since it wasn't an approved protest area, we figured our actions might actually prevent people from entering the plant since the police would be stationed elsewhere. So, about 5:00 in the morning we headed out, ready to lay nails, tacks and whatever other sharp objects across the road we could find. As we were placing two by fours spiked with large nails on the road, an Abalone organizer came over and started yelling at us for doing so. We were violating the agreement, she said. We told her we didn't give a fuck about the agreement but truly wanted to slow down the process in the hope that the reactor would not go online. As our argument attracted more attention, we decided to drop it since we weren't sure who was listening-police or protesters. The organizer removed our nail-laden boards from the road and gave them to one of the cops. Later in the morning, as we stood with our arms linked blocking the road and attempting to prevent buses and trucks carrying workers and materials for the plant from getting in, we were told not to fight back when the police attacked us. Southwester and I did anyhow and were scolded by other protesters for hurting our "brothers"-the police. Weird. The whole lot of us ended up in a makeshift jail for a few days while the demonstration continued at the plant.

The men's jail was really an unused military training camp that the state had cleaned up for the protest. We slept on mattresses on the floor and were guarded by National Guard reservists who had been called up for the duration of the action. I was allowed one shower during the four days I was there. The food consisted of sandwiches, raw vegetables, and some kind of powdered drink. Many of the detainees had never been in any kind of confinement before and did a hell of a lot of complaining about their rights. While I agreed with their arguments, I knew that the cops didn't really give a shit, so I thought it was wiser just to keep my mouth shut. It was better than a regular jailhouse, but it was still jail. While there, Wavy Gravy and the singer Jackson Browne gave an impromptu concert and talent show after one of the National Guard members called in to act as a jailer smuggled in his guitar from home. (The National Guard was mobilized for this action despite the promise made by then-Governor Jerry Brown at a rally the year before that he would only call out the Guard to keep the plant closed and never use them to lock up protesters).

Whenever a busload of protesters was brought in, we would greet them with a song or two-usually John

Lennon's "Power to the People" or the Beatles' "Yellow Submarine." Cecil Williams, who was the pastor of Glide Memorial Church in San Francisco and had a history of social protest and service, ran an ongoing seminar on social justice, nonviolent protest, violence and revolution. Nights were restless and, by the fourth day, quite rank smelling, thanks to the lack of showers, close quarters and daytime heat. When we finally went to court, everyone in our affinity group copped a plea just to get out of the detention center and back to Berkeley. The plant failed to go online on schedule. The delay was indirectly related to the protests and blockades: a group of scientists from a nearby university had discovered that the builders had read the blueprints incorrectly and had laid out parts of the plant the opposite of how it should have been. So the courts issued a delay while the plant was rebuilt.

Bedtime for Democracy

In July 1984, the Democrats came to San Francisco for their party convention. The soon-to-be-crowned nominee was Walter Mondale, a washed-up liberal who had grown increasingly irrelevant over the years. The left candidate, Jesse Jackson, had led his radical minions towards the center after a series of concerted media attacks tripped him up midway through the campaign and convinced him that he better stop vocalizing support for Palestine, democracy in Central America and his opposition to the Reagan foreign policy if he wanted to have any say in the Democrats' future.

In what has become standard practice in those cities chosen to host the major party political conventions, San Francisco had granted protesters a parking lot to protest in. The major difference between San Francisco and other cities was that the parking lot was actually near the convention center. For the most part, the rallies were tame. My friend Southwester and I headed over every day from Berkeley to sell "Nobody for President" stickers and take part in the protests. Usually by evening we found ourselves in a bar or park drinking a beer or two.

The afternoon of Mondale's nomination a network of anarchists and leftists staged a series of sit-ins and guerrilla theater actions in banks and corporate offices in the financial district. This was part of a protest designed to draw the connections between corporate America, its politicians and their policies of war and greed. This was the biggest and most exciting action of the week. By 3:00 PM, when the Dead Kennedys began playing their political punk rock on the main stage, close to four hundred protesters had been arrested. Two or three songs into the performance their lead singer, Jello Biafra, began to talk about the bust and urged people to head down to the Bryant Street jail after the concert. This is where those arrested were being held. Nazi skinheads attacked Jello during the next song. Other audience members pushed the skinheads off the stage and the band broke into their song "Nazi Punks Fuck Off."

Southwester and I joined the march after the concert. As several thousand of us headed towards the jail, plainclothes cops who looked like athletes in torn jeans began pulling the more vocal protesters out of the march and beating them. When other protesters saw this happening, they naturally rushed to defend their fellows, whether they knew the plainclothes perpetrators were cops or not. Of course, the cops then arrested these folks as well. By the time the crowd reached the jail, it had grown larger, but quieter. While we stood around yelling at the police, Walter Mondale was nominated to run against Ronald Reagan in November.

This summer and fall will bring the Democrats to Boston and the GOP to New York City for their nominating conventions. Planning groups are already working on strategies, permits and lodging for the multitude of protesters expected at both conventions. Of course, the Republicans are bound to have more opposition in the streets than the Democrats, if for no other reason than the confusion many people opposed to Bush have about calling the Democrats to task for their failure to provide any real alternative.

Both political parties and host cities, however, are doing their best to prevent protesters from having their say in a venue where the convention delegates will have to acknowledge them. Boston has proposed to the protest organizers that they set up shop in a small parking lot that is literally in the middle of a stack of freeways and surrounded by train tracks belonging to the city's subway/train system. If the courts decide against the city, one wonders how its police department will then respond? In other words, will the Boston police crack heads and preemptively arrest protesters if they can't stick them in some isolated part of the city. Given John Kerry's past as a protester, the outcome of this debate should prove interesting, to say the least. Like Robyn Blunter noted in a March 2, 2004 editorial for the St. Petersburg Times: "How is it that John Kerry, a veteran of the Vietnam War protest movement, is willing to stand by as constraints on dissent are proposed for the streets outside the convention where he will be nominated for president this summer?" Blumner fails to mention that Kerry was one of those who opposed the majority of his fellow Vietnam Veterans Against the War (VVAW) members when they refused to leave the Washington Mall in 1971 after the Nixon Justice department refused to grant the vets a permit to camp there. Still, his point is well taken.

As for the GOP and New York City: police, organizers and locals all expect tens of thousands of protesters outside this meeting. The police are already practicing for mass arrests and whatever else they are instructed to do to maintain the GOP's version of order.

According to organizers' websites, the police agencies involved have plans to create special zones within the city where the usual rights and liberties will be suspended. In addition, the authorities have stalled on issuing permits for several marches and have yet to answer in any way a request to let protesters sleep in one of the city parks. On top of this is the contrived show around the anniversary of 9-11. This in itself has been plenty of an excuse for the authorities to act outside their laws in the past. One can only assume that the presence of so many politicians, corporate bigwigs, and other GOP hangers-on will only intensify the authoritarian tendencies of those in the police state apparatus in New York's streets and high-rises.

People need to be ready. No matter what the courts decide regarding the issuance of permits and the like, there will be protests in Boston and New York. Boston must see protests because the Democrats should not be let off the hook just because they aren't Bush. The reasons for protests in New York do not even to be outlined. We should not let the authorities scare us away by using the courts against us. Nor should we allow their threats of chaos and disorder keep us away. Indeed, history makes it only too clear that it is the police and their bosses that create chaos and disorder, not the protesters. After the Chicago police were televised attacking and beating protesters outside the Democratic convention in August 1968, Mayor Daley (the elder) was quoted, "The police are not here to create disorder. The police are here to preserve disorder." Whether he meant to say this or not, its veracity remains. See you there.

Funeral For a Friend

There was this girl who showed up on Telegraph one spring. She had hair down to her ass and turquoise eyes, which was probably why she called herself Turquoise. Rube and I first met her one rainy evening while standing under an awning watching the rain. As she danced to the music in her head like some folks often do, she started talking. That's when we found out her name and that she liked my friend Jonny.

When Jonny saw her, he fell in love just like that. The next day they were sneaking off to the hills to make love in the sun. In a week they were sharing Jonny's room, and in two months, Turquoise was pregnant. Not long after that, they got married. Jonny's parents sent him some money, which was quite surprising since they had disowned him after he pawned some valuables of theirs when he was strung out on smack in the DC suburbs. Right after the wedding he received a check from the government, too. It seems that back in 1971 he'd been busted at the Mayday demonstrations against the war on the Capitol steps along with some bigshots (including some congresspeople and lawyers) who started a class action suit. Something about unconstitutional arrests during

Nixon's martial law. Ten years later, the courts decided against the government and Jonny was one of thousands who received 7500 dollars. He promptly invested in five pounds of killer Humboldt weed.

From there, he just took off. Soon he was dealing thirty or forty pounds a week plus a few thousand hits of acid. The baby came along and he and Turquoise seemed to be getting along pretty well. One thing about Jonny, though, was he loved mind altering experiences. There was a couple months there where we were doing ketamine enough so that our minds were never really connected to earth. Turquoise had a hard time with his experimentation but pretty much looked the other way. Or so it seemed. As time progressed their relationship had begun to get testy. Despite Jonny's stoic facade, the conflicts between he and Turquoise were tearing him up inside.

Jonny had a good acid dealing thing going where he was buying a couple grams of crystal LSD at a time and would make his own blotter. He was moving two grams of the shit a week. Unfortunately, as it turned out, his main assistant was Woody. Woody was a good enough guy but he loved junk. More than his kids, more than his mother, he loved junk. With all the money he and Jonny were rolling in, he was scoring some pretty pure stuff and he and Jonny were getting quite a jones. Still, somehow Jonny ended up doing himself in one afternoon at a motel in San Francisco. I guess he really needed the rest. Love is always the toughest. Humanity's lifelong challenge seems to be transcending its pain.

If previous tragedies hadn't convinced me, Jonny's death brought it home. Drugs had ceased to serve a liberatory function. After those first few years of revelation and communion, they were now just crutches or, even worse, tools of the oppressor. I knew this when acid and pot dealers I knew began considering guns a necessary tool of the profession. When old-time hippies who had always considered themselves providers of a sacrament began thinking only in terms of dollars, the signs were there. It didn't happen all at once to everyone (that first acid trip is still pretty revelatory, I bet), but the cultural changes we had fled from in the east were the first signs of the end. By the time I received that phone call up in Washington state telling me Jonny was dead, even pot and acid--the drugs we liked to call "life drugs"-- were tainted with the blood of the innocent. Much to the delight of those who never liked our culture in the first place. I remain convinced, however, that legalizing pot would go a long way to ending the abuse of some of the harder stuff for most people who choose to smoke marijuana.

Love and Work

I met Hope on Halloween, 1982. That night I found myself in a bar popular with college students and street types. She was sitting with a mutual friend from Massachusetts. I walked up, my face with a big star painted across it, and said, you must be Hope. She smiled and pulled back, not sure what to make of me in my Halloween finery. As for me, I was overwhelmed by her radiance. She had long, curly golden hair and the face of an angel. Although she generated innocence, there was an underlying current of sensuality that was impossible for me to ignore. I was pretty sure I was in love. After a few beers, the three of us left the bar. As Hope and her friend headed in another direction, she ran back and gave me a hug. A week later we made love and I knew this was one of those life changing moments. They really did happen.

A year or so later, a lot had changed. I was a father and working construction in order to get enough money to move out of Berkeley. Our destination was Washington State. We did eventually make it up to the Olympic Peninsula of Washington where, after a series of false leads and lies, we ended living in a double-wide trailer in the woods at the back of a friend's land near the town of Shelton. Shelton was a backwater town whose main industry was logging. The Simpson Timber Company built it up to do its work and, now that its work was almost done there, it was letting the town fall apart. The only businesses in town making money other than the grocery store were the bars and the churches—two establishments which feed off of depression and misery. A couple real estate agencies weren't doing too bad either selling off prime lakeshore property to folks making good in the Seattle computer industry.

The area we lived in was beautiful. There was a lake at the back end of the property where the mist rose off each morning. The trail through the rainforest to the water was bordered by salal, trillium, and dozens of other wildflowers. Right before the last clump of fir trees on the lakeshore was a field which turned yellow in the spring when the hundreds of daffodils bloomed. Our young son's favorite place in these woods was a small grove of red cedars where the ground underneath was covered in several inches of cedar needles. This environment made our lives bearable.

I found a tedious job assembling circuit boards for a company which could underbid similar firms by virtue of its cheap labor costs. These costs were low because of the changes then occurring in the lumber business and the consequent large numbers of mill workers and loggers being laid off or forced into early retirement by the trend towards offshore milling and the plain fact that the number of harvestable forests was rapidly dwindling due to the practice of clearcutting. At any rate, while the former employees of Simpson Timber collected unemployment, their wives, live-in lovers, and adult children supplemented the family income with their minimum wage jobs. As far as improving our lot as workers at the company, the unemployment in the region combined with the yellow dog clause against union organizing written into our contracts effectively frightened everyone away from that route.

The fellow we rented our trailer from was a part-time carpenter and a full time pot grower. All the pot he grew was grown indoors under halide lights. After Hope left that summer I helped him out. It was under his tutelage that my horticultural skills were developed. The herb was extremely high quality. I had no interest in the sale aspect of the project so I was paid in a small percentage of the crop—enough to keep me high when I wanted to be. Because of the depressed economics of the region, we were but one of the thousands of pot growers in the region. People who had hated pot smokers not more than fifteen years ago had turned to the crop as a means of paying their mortgage or keeping food on their tables. The absurdity of pot prohibition was very apparent as previously law abiding folks whose cleverness failed them were sent to prison for longer terms for growing weed than people convicted of rape or murder.

Papa Bush Starts a War

The crowd at Olympia's Sylvester Park on January 15, 1991 exceeded our expectations. Even the police expressed their surprise at the large numbers and enthusiasm. By the time the speakers had begun, there were more than 3000 people in the park and the streets surrounding it. Curtis and I ran interference—keeping folks off the stage and helping keep order among the scheduled speakers. Susan introduced the participants and Anna kept the show moving. The only conflict that arose on stage was when Democratic Congresswoman Jolene Unsoeld approached us and asked to speak. Curtis and I were against such a move, not because we had anything in particular against her, but because we did not want politicians diluting our message or riding our coattails. Anna and some others felt just as strongly the other way. Eventually, Curtis and I gave in, knowing that the final speech would be given by Peter Bohmer in front of the Capitol and there was no doubt about his stance. Within days Unsoeld was supporting the war under the guise of supporting the troops, like so many other politicians.

After the rally ended, a group of drummers organized by Mike O. went into the street and waited while people lined up behind them. Then the crowd headed up Capitol Way to the Capitol. The police did a little pushing and shoving but for the most part they behaved themselves. After the majority of the crowd had reached the parking lot in front of the Capitol, Peter began to speak. He gave a rousing twenty minute talk tying together the fight for justice and against imperial war and then urged everyone to join him inside the Capitol where we would attempt to present a petition demanding the Washington State Legislature pass a resolution opposing a war against Iraq. People headed towards the doors. As they went inside police asked them to leave their signs at the door. Once inside, the chant "No War!" began in earnest once again. While most of us remained in the rotunda, about 500 protesters went looking for a door into the chambers. Eventually they found one and streamed into the room. The Legislature had closed early that day because of the demonstration and the room was empty. Not for long, though. Soon, close to a thousand people were in the room, chanting, talking, and dancing. Some of the more organized members of the crowd began to strategize a plan for the longer term. They called the group to some kind of order and expressed their desire to occupy the chambers until the legislators responded to the proposed resolution. Meanwhile the police were gathering their forces and talking to each other on walkie-talkies. The press was sending out their version of the events on the national wire and over the television airwaves via CNN.   Within the hour, news of the action had spread and more media were streaming in as protesters began to settle in for a long stay. By dark most folks had left the chambers. Some headed home. Most, however, joined a vigil and prayer session that had begun an hour earlier in the Capitol rotunda.

Around 9:00 pm, while the speeches and praying went on in the rotunda of the Washington State Capitol building in Olympia, a different type of action was playing out in the chambers– by now sealed off by state troopers and a variety of other law enforcement types— where a dozen or so protesters from the earlier celebration/takeover continued their occupation and protest against the impending attack against Iraq. Capitol grounds administrators and police talked back and forth about physically removing the people inside. Myself and one or two other organizers asked them to hold off. Meanwhile we waited for attorney John Thorne to return an earlier phone call. Although John could not legally practice in the state, he had plenty of experience dealing with police in all types of situations. His experience in California during the sixties and seventies representing everyone from a police union in San Jose to the revolutionary George Jackson insured that. On top of that, he had helped us deal with the police during other protests in Olympia against American policy, including showing up at a moment's notice after a confrontation following a 1989 protest against US policy in El Salvador and retrieving my friend David from jail. This would be child's play.

After finding the room where the police were planning their move, John began asking around for the officer in charge. At first, none of the police wanted to talk to him, but after he told them he was an attorney, a lieutenant eventually materialized. After brief introductions, John and the lieutenant left the hallway to discuss the protesters who were locked in the chambers. Meanwhile, I waited. So did the troopers. When John came back, he winked at me, shook the lieutenant's hand and we headed upstairs to the lobby and the continuing vigil.

144

"They're going to let them stay the night, Ron." Said John, referring to the demonstrators inside the chambers. "As long as they leave in the morning. Do you think they'll go for it?"

"Probably." I said. "If we can get some food in to them."

"Anyone working on that?" asked Thorne.

"Yeah. The co-op people put together some sandwiches and have them outside in a truck."

By this time, we had arrived at the locked doors of the chambers and began to knock rather loudly. The food co-op workers were already there with a box of sandwiches and drinks. After a minute or two, Ceridwen, one of the occupiers, opened the door a crack and peered out. We assured her that no police were around. She then opened the door wide enough for the box of food to be handed to her. After a quick word or two of assurance regarding their overnight stay, I went back to the vigil where a group of teenagers were harassing another teenager for wearing the US flag as a headband.

The following day, the local daily *The Olympian*, like the television media, treated the Capitol protest as spectacle. This angered me. In a conversation with

Symphonox a week or two later regarding this recurrent tendency of the media to portray all events as spectacles that just seem to happen without organization or any other type of forethought, he asked me, rather sarcastically, what could we do about it. The question stopped me for a moment. After all, we didn't want to organize a spectacle, we wanted to organize a movement. Yet if the media insisted on portraying our work as spectacle, it was up to us to figure out how to use their portrayal as an organizing tool. We couldn't play just to the media, yet we shouldn't ignore it either. In union organizing, one can ignore the media since the union's audience is in the workplace and composed of folks the organizers know. But we weren't organizing a union, we were organizing a movement against imperial war. There was no way we could reach everyone we wanted to reach without letting the mainstream media do some of the talking. The trick was to create events and information that the corporate media could not reinterpret to fit their bosses' needs. Little did some of us know that soon even that opportunity would be denied as the media just stopped reporting any opposition to the war at all.

When I arrived at work the next morning it was eerie. The first thing I was reminded of was the Gary Cooper movie "High Noon" where everyone knows a big shootout is coming, but nobody wants to deal with it. So we just went about our work as if nothing was too out of the ordinary.

After work, I headed up to the elementary school to get my son Ian. We walked back down Capitol Way as we usually did and stopped in at a bakery shop where we often bought an after school snack. After Ian had made a selection, I handed the young woman at the counter a five dollar bill. As she was making change, the music on the radio was interrupted by one of those special news bulletins. Baghdad had been attacked. As Peter Arnett's disembodied voice related the events, we could hear the sound of explosions in the background. The young woman began to cry and set down my change. I reached over to grab it and she grabbed my hand. I gripped her hand tightly until the fellow working in the kitchen appeared. He hugged her and she let go her grip. Ian and I hurried out the door and headed for a pay phone. I needed to call others in the coalition to get ready for the protest we knew was going to happen. Despite our hopes, we knew that there would be a war and had planned, like most other similar groups throughout the world, a meeting time and place once the opening salvos were fired. In Olympia, that place was Sylvester Park and the time was approximately 6:00 PM the day the shooting began.

We ate a quick dinner and went to Sylvester Park where a crowd was already gathering. Curtis showed up soon after we arrived, as did Anna, Tracy, Michael, Harry and Grace from the Citizen's Band, and several other active OAIC organizers. While we tried to get ourselves together, a radio blasted live reports from Baghdad, D.C., and other spots around the world, reporting news and repeating rumors.

The emotions of the crowd (by now around 1000) in the park vacillated between fear, anger and distress. All of which added to an ever growing sense of urgency and a desire to react immediately without much forethought. Up on the gazebo stage, Curtis rounded up people willing to serve as a nominal security group. Their primary purpose would be to link arms around the speakers and musicians as they appeared and hopefully prevent any attacks from unfriendly elements. Meanwhile, Anna negotiated furiously for a sound system while Harry and Grace wondered where theirs was. We had been told it was on its way a half hour earlier.

After another ten minutes, our adhoc group decided we shouldn't wait any longer. Since I had the voice which could carry the furthest, I was chosen to lead off the rally. I stepped to face the crowd just as the van carrying the sound system arrived. The crowd's attention turned to me as I began.

"Hello." I began. "I grew up in a military family and spent most of my youth on or near military bases. When I was eight years old my dad was assigned to Peshawar in what was then West Pakistan. While we lived there, the governments of India and Pakistan went to war over a piece of land known as Kashmir. As Americans, my friends and I didn't think too much about it, but were a little fascinated by the goings on around us: windows painted black and nightly blackouts, air raid drills, warplanes flying overhead. " I continued with a brief synopsis of those days in Pakistan when the war raged around us. Then I went ahead.

"Four years later, I was living in the States again and my dad was sent to Vietnam to fight in another war. I didn't want him to go and I didn't want him to be involved in the killing. My family was lucky—much luckier than thousands of other families both Vietnamese and American—he came back intact. While he was away, my mom gave birth to my second-youngest sister. If dad had died over there, he would never have known her and her cheerful, spirited self. Like many other families, the war drove a wedge between my father and us older kids. I feared the day I would have to face the draft and did my damnedest to get that war over. We were fortunate—we did end that war, but only after way too many had died. Only after way too much had been destroyed.

Now, as we stand here other soldiers are carrying out an attack with horrific weapons on people of another country in our name. Already radio reports speak of thousands dead. Whether it's thousands or just one, it's too many. This suffering must end. This war must end. And we must help end it.

Our struggle will not be easy. At times, we will want to quit. At times we will question the point of our resistance. But we must never quit. No! We must raise our level of opposition to a greater level then. Sometimes we will offend some folks, maybe even our family or friends. Sometimes we will be verbally abused or physically assaulted. We must not, no, can not, give in. Like the great fighter for the liberation of black people in this country from slavery , Frederick Douglas, said:

If there is no struggle, there is not progress. Those who profess to favor freedom, yet deprecate agitation, are men who want crops without plowing up the ground. They want rain without the thunder and lightning. They want the ocean without the awful roar of its many waters. This struggle may be a moral one; or it may be a physical one; or it may be both mental and physical; but it must be a struggle. Power concedes nothing without a demand.

About midway through the speech, the PA system was connected and I no longer needed to shout. As soon as I finished Harry and Grace played a tune. After that, other members of the crowd said a few words. While this went on, a truck full of war supporters drove by and threw some bricks into the crowd. Fortunately no one was seriously hurt. By 8:30, many folks in the crowd were emotionally spent. Those of us on the stage who were more or less managing the rally decided to go ahead with a suggestion by members of the crowd to march through the downtown streets, come back to the park and call it a night. Curtis and I remained behind. After the last protester left the park we went across the street and drained a couple quick beers.

Harry and Grace had not bothered to go on the march since someone needed to watch the sound equipment so we brought them back some coffee. The four of us dissembled the PA and made plans to be back the next day for an even larger demonstration and possible occupation of the Federal Building. When the crowd returned to the park, I shouted out that announcement and wished everyone a decent night's sleep.

Waiting for the Last War to End

It was a particularly rainy day for the Pacific Northwest, even for February. Instead of the normal heavy mist that one thought of in the same way one thinks of the muzak in a shopping mall, the rain on this day was heavy and unrelenting. Indeed, it was even a topic of conversation-which rain rarely ever was in this land of the temperate rainforest.

Consequently, Hali and I were keeping close to the center of the gazebo in Olympia's Sylvester Park in order to stay dry. Most of our leaflets and newspapers were still in the plastic bags we stored them in and nobody had come to visit us in the two hours we had been sitting there. So Hali and I shared hitchhiking stories and tales of chemically-fueled experiences that had taken us to other realms. Then Tommy showed up.

"Hey, y'all," he said. "What's up? I'm fuckin' wet as a goddam baby fresh out of her mama's womb." He used his cane to climb up the bandstand stairs and get out of the weather. Once he was at the top, he sat down on a bench we had retrieved from the park for the day and begin to use his handkerchief to dry his face.

Tommy was a vet who had lost some use of his leg in Vietnam when he was hit by shrapnel. After

153

recuperating from his wound in a California hospital he had returned to his mother's house somewhere in the American south and went to college. That had lasted for a year or two before he got the urge to travel. Once he hit the road that was it.

He was sold on the life of the vagabond. Like many of his fellow road warriors, he liked to drink. Unlike many of them, though, he was a quiet and peaceful drinker. He had begun coming to the antiwar demonstrations the previous October, holding a sign he had drawn himself. Until the big protest on January 15th, he was usually the only African-American man in the crowd. Today, he was drinking his favorite-peach brandy. Once he settled in on the bench, he cracked his bottle and offered Hali and I a nip. I took advantage of the offer.

"So what do you guys have lined up next?" he asked. Tommy hated meetings so he counted on us for updates about the coalition.

Hali began, "We're gonna' hold a silent funeral procession from here to the Capitol in a week or so. Once we get to the Capitol grounds we're gonna' hold a mock funeral for all those killed in this stupid war."

"I'm there." He replied. "Anything I can do to help? Like draw some signs or something?" His artwork, while primitive, was powerful and direct. He handed me the bottle again. I took a longer swallow this time around. It was getting pretty fuckin' cold sitting in the rain.

"Man, it's freezing." I said. Hali moved closer and shared the blanket she was using to keep warm with me.

"You want some, Tommy?" she asked.

"No man. I'm cool. This coat I got at the shelter is plenty warm. Thanks anyhow." He pulled his pocket radio out of the small daypack he always carried. "Let me find out what the weatherman is saying. Maybe we gonna' get some snow."

Tommy turned on the radio and searched for a station. He stopped on one of the rock stations from Seattle that happened to be playing "Give Peace A Chance."

"Wow. I'm surprised to hear that on commercial radio." remarked Hali. "The DJ's boss must be away." The airwaves were full of nationalistic nonsense ever since the war had begun and the audience was eating it up. Tommy took another nip and the radio began playing "What's Going On" by Marvin Gaye. As the song reached the second chorus, I noticed the rain had stopped.

"I'm gonna' go," I said. "It's not raining and I need to go to work in a couple hours. See y'all." Hali gave me a kiss on the cheek and Tommy shook my hand. I ran towards the bus stop at the corner of the park. Before the rain began again, the bus came and I got on.

The war continued. Hali, Tommy and others from our antiwar group continued our protest.

The west has always been the European settler's golden land of the great frontier. And, according to ancient Egyptian myth, the west is also the land where the souls of the dead go to live again. If this is true, I'm not sure what that makes the eastern shores, other than the place where we were before we went west. The seat of financial and political power in the United States, the east is also where many of our families first began. It was this latter reality that may have been what pulled me back after so many years out west. The trick was finding a place where a sense of openness like that found on the west coast existed. Vermont seemed to fit the bill. A stubbornly rural state populated with old time Yankees who could face down any winter and refugees from the metropolises of the east, the politics are unique in comparison to most of the rest of the US two party dictatorship. This created a strong independent movement that was somewhat hijacked by politicians like Bernie Sanders and Jim Jeffords-- moves that have confused many citizens but encouraged others to look beyond the limits of the electoral system and attempt grassroots movements with varying degrees of success.

Then there's the fact of Vermont's whiteness. Although its non-white population has grown considerably over the past fifteen years, it remains one of the whitest states in the union. This does not mean there are no poor folks, since class is a sociological fact no matter where one lives. I does mean, however, that Vermonters oftentimes don't get it when it comes to cultures that are not derivatives of those from Europe.

Once Again, Mr. Congressman, War Is Not a Humanitarian Act!

On April 26, 1999, a rally and march were held in Burlington, Vermont, USA against the U.S. war on Yugoslavia. Approximately 100 people (mostly local high school and college students along with some veteran activists including Dave Dellinger) attended the 45 minute rally at the University of Vermont campus and then marched down Main Street. The destinations of the march were the local offices of Vermont's three congressional members: Senators Leahy (Dem.) and Jeffords (Rep.), and Rep. Bernie Sanders. All of these men currently support the bombing of Yugoslavia. The purpose of these visits was to present petitions calling for "an immediate end to the bombing, a return to the negotiating table... and no introduction of NATO ground forces to the conflict". The 1,000 signatures on these petitions were collected in a little over two weeks time.

At Senator Leahy's office, a small delegation of demonstrators went into the office, presented the petitions and were served cookies. At Senator Jeffords' office, the delegation that went inside asked for and received a conference call with Mr. Jeffords' foreign policy advisor in Washington, D.C.. From there, we headed to Bernie Sanders' office at the top of Burlington's downtown pedestrian mall (Church Street). Once we arrived at the office building , the remaining protesters (approximately 30 in all) headed inside and up the stairs to Sanders' office. We were met by his staff who presented us with a written statement by Mr. Sanders concerning his support of the bombing. Those present read the statement and then asked a member of the staff if we could hold a conference call with Bernie and give him a chance to justify his position. We were told this was not possible because Sanders was on a plane to Washington, D.C. and he did not own a cell phone. So we sat down and informed the staff that we would wait until we could speak with Sanders.

Seattle musician Jim Page happens to be in Burlington this week and accompanied us on the march. While we sat in the office, he played guitar and sang songs in between discussions about the war, the killings in Littleton, CO., the arrogance of liberals in power and numerous other subjects took place. As time passed, it became clear that Bernie had no intention of talking to us. After conversations out of our earshot, the primary staffperson informed us that we could meet with Bernie next Tuesday if we made an appointment. This suggestion was rejected out of hand; the reasoning being that hundreds more would die in the interim. Time ticked on.

Around 5:30 PM, we were asked again if we wanted to accept the meeting with Bernie next Tuesday. We agreed to the meeting but also insisted on speaking with Sanders that day. Furthermore, we affirmed that we would not leave the office until we spoke with Bernie that evening. We were than told that our choice was to either leave then and meet with Sanders next week or stay until we were removed and not meet with the congressmen at all. At 6:00 PM or so, we were asked once again if we would assent to this arrangement. Once again we said no. At 6:45 PM, Burlington police officers began arresting those protesters who refused to leave when asked. This was done at the request of Congressman Sanders and his staff. The arrests were conducted in an orderly fashion and all were released later in the evening.

This was the first time Sanders office had ever been occupied. One has to wonder if it will be the last.

Locked Out and Pissed Off

As I flew into DC's National Airport Wednesday night, I could see celebratory fireworks over near the Washington Monument. It was the beginning of the Bush version of a party-something akin to Nero fiddling while Rome burned. Of course, I couldn't help but think of the much more dangerous explosions that are daily occurrences in the Iraq that Washington's war has made. After retrieving my backpack form the baggage claim, I made my way to the Metro station, purchased a farecard and got on the next train. The first thing I noticed was the numerous white women wearing fur coats and hanging tight to their tuxedo clad husbands. Not your usual subway crowd by any means. Apparently, the three inch snowfall in DC that day had screwed up the schedules of these celebrants' limousines. Ah, the sufferings of the rich and powerful.

Thursday morning I headed into DC from the place I was staying in Maryland. After a series of public transportation holdups, I finally got to the area of the city where the inauguration was being held. Talk about lockdown. Everywhere one looked there was fencing and security personnel. DC police, Secret Service, FBI,

National Guard and active duty military-all of them very well-armed. In addition to the folks on the ground, every government building along the route had a half-dozen sharpshooters on its roof. Because of the extreme security measures, one had to walk several blocks out of the way in order to reach their destination. After walking at least two miles out more than would have been necessary under normal circumstances, I finally reached an access point to the Mall where folks were gathered to listen to W's speech. Now, the way the Bush people had the entry points into their security zone set up, one had to already have a ticket to enter through most of them. Most of these tickets were provided to those who had worked or donated to the Bush campaign and the rest were sold prior to the date. The rest of us-protesters and supporters alike-had but one point of entry. Of course, the lines were extremely long and, once one got to the front, they were subject to a patdown search. By the time I had gone through this exercise and entered the Mall grounds, Bush was beginning his speech. To be honest, I didn't listen to much of it, choosing instead to observe the crowd, which seemed to be made up of several dozen groups of high school students in the general area where I stood.

The Mall itself was less than half full of people. Recent antiwar demonstrations have drawn more people.

I left the area after Bush's promise to end tyranny (one assumes his definition of tyranny doesn't include the governments in DC, Tel Aviv, or Iraq). From there I began to make my way over to a decent vantage point from which to watch the parade. In addition, I was looking for some likeminded folks. I have never been in DC and felt like I was in such an alien environment. The vanilla suburbs had truly invaded the chocolate city, to borrow the terminology of George Clinton. It was somewhat disconcerting. After walking another couple of miles to cover what would normally have been a six or seven-block walk, I reached the back of the White House. There was the tail end of an earlier antiwar demonstration remaining there. Most of the people involved were participating in a die-in in sympathy with the people of Iraq. One male Bush supporter stopped and asked me what was going on. I told him and he responded: "Gee, they look like me after the party last night." Despite his trivialization of the matter, I admit I had to laugh at his joke.

Then I wandered on, eventually reaching the intersection of 14th and F Streets. There was a large crowd of protesters there. This was a crowd made up of mostly young and exuberant folks who were not attached to any particular organization. Some were identified as anarchists, some as socialists, some as Democrats and some just folks. They were waiting in line to get through the security points, others were chanting slogans in the street, and still others were arguing with Bush supporters walking by. I remembered the intersection and walked on, intending to find the rest of the antiwar folks who were assembled under the auspices of the ANSWER coalition. I walked all the way to 3rd and C Streets, where the ANSWER folks were trying to get in. There was a long line and the process was very slow. Making a split-second decision, I decided to go back up to 14th Street and spend my afternoon there.

The security situation at this point was this: there were three fences; in between the first and second fence stood a tight row of DC police in full riot gear; in between the second and third fence (which stood directly behind the viewing bleachers) stood a more loosely-organized line of security forces, some in camouflage with automatic weapons and some in plainclothes. As the day wore on, the sense of being purposely excluded frustrated and angered the crowd of several thousand on the two blocks of 14th Street more and more. A couple of young people burned a US flag while some nationalist clown dressed in red, white and blue attempted to wrestle with them. Protesters engaged in shouting matches with overly smug Bush supporters dressed in fur coats and tuxedos. The insults from the Bushites were familiar: get a job, move to Iraq, and so on. Eventually, as the frustration of the protesters continued to grow, virtually all sense of decorum left the crowd. Taunts from Bush supporters were met with the simple response (recently popularized once again by Dick Cheney) of "Go fuck yourself." Young and old protesters utilized this repeatedly throughout the afternoon. More and more riot cops poured into the street as more protesters showed up and grew rowdier.

The old Willard Hotel takes up a block of 14th Street between F and G. Its front steps stood about fifty feet away from the first security fence and also gave folks the closest view of the parade from the outside of the security zone. By 3 PM this area was filled with protesters, some of them intent on tearing down the security fence. As they disengaged various sections of the fence (only to have them put back in place by the cops), the riot squad began spraying some kind of pepper tear gas. Various demonstrators responded by pelting the cops with snowballs, who then sprayed more gas. By the time Cheney and then Bush's cars were announced, the crowd near the hotel was angry and loud and some, even through our scarves and bandannas we held over our faces to lessen the effects of the gas. After this part of the parade passed, folks began to filter away from the front of the hotel but not away from the protest. In response, the riot cops began to add reinforcements with the intention of clearing the streets.

One note about the DC police. In a scenario reminiscent of a colonial army made up of local nationals (think the new Iraqi National Guard), it appears that the majority of the men and women who make up DC's riot squad are Black. This was not the case thirty years ago, but it is today. In short, the wealthy white folks of Washington's corporate war establishment have a bunch of non-white skinned folks protecting their buildings and their right to oppress. The irony is not lost.

Various skirmishes between the riot squad and the protesters continued throughout the rest of the afternoon. I personally only witnessed one arrest. However, there were probably more. After leaving DC that evening, I went to my parents' house in Maryland and talked politics with my dad. He asked why I was protesting. My response was simple: Never have I felt so locked out of this nation's so-called democratic process. Suffice it to say, the day's events reinforced that perception in a very real and physical manner.

A20 in Washington, DC--Bringing the Message to the Beast's Belly

This was a demonstration I had to attend. The madmen running the world were in a severe state of psychosis and threatening to take us all down with them. I'd made plans to be on one of the buses going to DC a few weeks ago. Then Ariel Sharon unleashed his military assault on the people in the Occupied Territories, killing civilians left and right, trashing their homes, schools, churches, marketplaces and anything else that his "moral" army felt like trashing in the name of colonial expansion. I knew I had to go and there was nothing short of a catastrophic illness that would prevent me. So I hopped on the bus the night of April 19th.

Speaking of the Israeli invasion of Palestine. Rumors of dissension in the organizers' ranks of one of the primary organizations putting this protest together over Israel's actions had filtered up to us in the northern lands. Supposedly, there were those in the A20Stop the War coalition who didn't want to condemn Israel's death and destruction, considering this violation of every human right justified. If this was true, it meant that once again the Zionist apologists in the peace

169

movement were attempting to convince the rest of us that any war Israel fought was not to be considered a war. How this dynamic works I have never been certain. What's good for the USA goose is also good for the Israeli gander if you ask me. Wars of expansion are wars of expansion. Israel is the US bulldog in the Middle East, no matter what we are told about it being the other way around. Israel is immorally occupying territories with US funds and support in violation of international law. If the situation were reversed, one could be damn certain that the US would be calling for war against the Palestinian invaders. To use Washington's reasoning, Israel's occupation of Palestine is as illegal as Iraq's 1990 occupation of Kuwait. Yet, of course, US bombers are not bombing Tel Aviv.

On Friday the 19th of April, I showed up at the meeting place we had been given by the Burlington AntiWar Coalition. Dozens of other folks were there, as were two chartered buses and several vans. Young and old and representing a variety of concerns ranging from peace to opposition to capitalist globalization, we talked amongst ourselves until the drivers were ready. Then we boarded our vehicles and headed into the Vermont night. Our bus stopped at three more Vermont towns to pick up another three dozen protesters before we hit the open highway. All in all, close to two hundred Vermonters traveled in this set of arranged rides. Probably another hundred or so went down in their own vehicles or on other forms of transport.

After a ten hour ride that went smoothly except for a bit of a slowdown around New York City due to road work taking place on the George Washington Bridge, we disembarked at the New Carrolton Metro stop-a mere six stops from the Federal Triangle-a point almost in the center of where the four feeder rallies were to occur. Once out of the metro, I bought a coffee or two and headed over to the Ellipse with Will Miller and few other compatriots. This was where the largest of the scheduled opening rallies was to be held. It was sponsored by the ANSWER coalition (Act Now to Stop War and End Racism)-a loose- knit coalition of antiwar, anti-imperialist, anti-racist, and Palestinian support organizations organized under the auspices of the International Action Center.

The other three rallies were organized somewhat along these lines: A20Stop the War-a coalition of peace and youth groups originally called by the Youth and Student Mobilization for Peace and Justice, the

Mobilization for Global Justice-an adhoc conglomeration of groups opposed to capitalist globalization featuring many of the folks and groups involved in every anti- capitalist rally from Seattle on, and the Palestine Solidarity Coalition- exactly what it sounds like, this rally was organized by groups in support of the liberation of Palestine from the Zionist government of Israel. Somewhat secular in nature, it espoused many of the same demands as those put forth at the ANSWER rally.

Anyhow, our group arrived at the ANSWER rally on the Ellipse and made plans to meet back up later. I headed off to make my rounds of the literature tables that were springing up on the edge of the growing crowd. When I first arrived I estimated approximately 3000 people had preceded me. As I wandered around, more and more protesters streamed into the sunny green just south of the White House. Some carried signs opposing the war on Afghanistan and Colombia. Other signs called for an end to the detention of the those rounded up in the wake of 911 and in Camp Xray in Cuba. Still others had buttons spoofing the idiocy of GW Bush and the Puritan fascism of John Ashcroft. The dominant symbol of the day, however, were the

Palestinian flags, stickers, and t-shirts that simply said Free Palestine. It was becoming obvious that this day was going to be one of those times when the events in the world superseded any plans the organizers may have had-the demand for a liberated Palestine was going to be the order of the day. The blatant disregard for the humanity of the Palestinians by Israel's army in the past weeks had finally been enough. People in the United States were going to address this issue and bring it home that the occupation and its terror would no longer be ignored.

The people just kept coming. Muslim families with the women in full burqa from Islamic centers and mosques around the country, young Arab and Arab-American men and women dressed in the current style of American teenagers with the red, black, green and white Palestinian flag tied around their neck like a cape, African-Americans wearing the red, black and green of Africa on their shirt and a small Palestinian flag stuck in their headgear, Asian-Americans, Latinos, members of Jewish congregations carrying signs opposing the occupation, and lots of white folk. They just kept streaming in, occasionally breaking out in chants, with the most popular being Free, Free Palestine and End the

Occupation, Now! Occasionally one heard Allah Akbar-God is Great, or a modified version of one of the standard antiwar chants. The sound came and went like waves in the steamy heat. I think I can accurately state that I have never been at an antiwar rally in this country where there were so many shades of skin tone and cultures represented.

The speeches began around 11 AM and, after a few of them, I decided to go check out the other rallies. This wasn't because I didn't want to hear at least some of the speakers, especially Pakistani writer and activist Tariq Ali, but because I had vowed to attend as many of the feeder rallies as possible. So I headed over to the Sylvan Theatre near the Washington Monument, which is where the rally sponsored by the A20 Stop the War Coalition was going on. As I ambled over in that direction I noticed a stage with perhaps 500 people gathered around it. This was the so-called Patriot's rally. It was sponsored by a right-wing group calling itself the Free Republic and, from what I could hear, spent most of its time labeling the antiwar/anti-capitalist protesters "parasites" and quoting George Washington and Tom Paine in a context that gave new and most likely unintended meaning to these men's words. Interestingly enough, as I had moved out of hearing distance of the ANSWER rally, I heard George Washington being quoted there, too. The ANSWER speaker was referring to Washington's warnings against the potential for tyranny by government. At day's end, the only thing one could honestly say about this so- called Patriot's rally was that it had the best sound system and the smallest crowd.

Walking past the lines of tourists waiting to get into the Washington Monument and the new concrete barriers all around the structure, I began to hear a reggae beat emanating from the A20 Stop the War Coalition stage. Upon reaching the rally site, I was struck immediately by two things-the smell of burning sage and the difference in the rally's makeup. There was a much higher percentage of young people, which stood to make sense since one the original members of the coalition was a nationwide youth and student organization founded in the wake of 911 and devoted to opposing war and terrorism. In addition, there were many older pacifists in the crowd, at the tables around the edges and on the stage. This was a more traditional US peace rally-mostly white-skinned, mostly younger, and mostly middle-class. Nothing wrong with that, for sure, but a remarkable contrast to the gathering a few hundred meters away. I wandered the crowd of 20,000 or so looking for familiar faces and listening to the music for another 30 minutes. Then I headed towards the Palestine Solidarity Rally. This rally was about a mile further on near Dupont Circle, which is in the Georgetown District of DC. Unfortunately I never made it to the rally, for, as I was heading that way, I saw a march leaving from the rally site and headed towards the A20 Stop the War rally. Apparently, these two groups were to meet up there and then converge with the ANSWER rally on Pennsylvania Avenue. Assuming that since I had missed one feeder rally already and that I would probably miss the other one called by the anti-capitalist demonstrators who were in town to protest the war and the IMF/World Bank spring meetings occurring that weekend, I headed back to the ANSWER rally, hoping to catch the last few speakers.

When I got back to this rally it had more than doubled in size. There were easily 50,000 people in the Ellipse and more were still streaming in. As buses from all over the country parked and their passengers disembarked, the crowd grew larger and louder. It was pretty much impossible to hear the speakers. Too bad we couldn't have ripped off the sound system from the right- winger's rally across the way. From my vantage point near the southeast corner of the Ellipse, I could see both the ANSWER and the A20 Stop the War rallies. As I listened to clerics from Islamic, Jewish and Christian churches, temples and mosques express solidarity and support for Palestine and offer a prayer to the God of Abraham, I watched marchers from the anti-capitalist and Palestinian solidarity march converge with the participants of the A20 Stop the War rally. As these folks begin to line up in 14th street, the clerics held their joined hands together in a jubilant celebration of humanity's possibilities. Then, we began to line up on 14th Street ourselves. By the time all the marches had converged near the corner of 14th and Pennsylvania, the march itself stood forty abreast and several city blocks long. The chants of Free Palestine! End the Occupation! and with calls for an end to the terrorism of the US "war on terrorism" and money for social services and rebuilding instead of war were heard throughout Washington, DC. Each corner where the march turned was guarded by police two rows deep, some on horses and some on motorcycles-all of them in full riot gear, yet with their visors back and many with smiles on their faces. It was loud, it was large and it was amazing. I had not been at a demonstration this spirited and large since one I attended in 1974 demanding Richard Nixon's impeachment.

I stood on a small hill for ten minutes watching the parade. I never saw the beginning or the end of it while on that perch. I figured there were easily 75,000 to 100,000 participants. There were probably more, since the mainstream media and park police put in estimates of 70,000 and they are notorious for underestimating crowds of this nature. Either way, the events of this day marked a turning point in the history of the Palestinian and American peoples. Never again will the Palestinians wonder if they have friends in the United States. This march and others like it around the country have proven to them that they do. Furthermore, the tremendous diversity of philosophies- political and religious-amongst the people who participated (and those that were there in spirit) showed the world that Washington's war on the world is not popular here either. As a young friend and organizer summed it up on the bus back to Vermont: "This was an awesome beginning to what can be an awesome movement for freedom and justice." I say, "Let's roll."

Would Ethan Allen Pay to Protest?

I left Burlington, Vermont in June 2005. After twelve years there, leaving was bittersweet at best. Having grown up as a military brat, twelve years was the longest that I had ever lived in one town consecutive years, plus Vermont is an incredibly tolerant place. In fact, with the exception of its bitterly cold winters, it would be ideal. Politically, it tends towards a libertarian communitarianism--a combination of New England independence/live-and-let-live philosophy born in the muskets of Ethan Allen and his Green Mountain Boys and their fight for independence and against monied land speculators from New York and Britain. This belief is complemented by a general assumption that every resident deserves a decent shelter and food on the table. This combination of independence and social welfare is part of the reason that Bernie Sanders gets reelected every two years as the state's congressperson.

I always thought that part of the reason for Vermont's generally progressive social and economic policies stemmed from its small size. As of 2000, there were only around 500,000 residents. Now, that's less than one-third the number of people who live in

Manhattan spread out over almost 300 times the area. Even in Burlington--the state's largest and most densely populated city--this means that there is a lot of room to move around. In addition, the small population breeds a familiarity. One can walk down Burlington's Church Street pedestrian mall and get into an argument with Bernie Sanders or the mayor if they so desire. In addition, the relative amount of room each individual has tends to make people feel quite comfortable and even relaxed. Manhattan seems to do the opposite to most folks.

The history of progressive politics of modern Vermont comes from a combination of factors. Foremost among them would be the influx of counterculture and new leftist types during the late 1960s and the 1970s--refugees from the Nixonian reality of the Northeast cities in the era of Kent State and Watergate. Additional elements are the numbers of liberal thinking young professionals who moved to the area in the 1980s and 1990s, along with the ever expanding lesbian and gay population. The latter population enjoys the relative tolerance and acceptance that they find in the state, especially after Vermont became the first state to recognize civil unions between same sex couples. Of course, one must still have a desire to live in a basically rural environment [i.e., live five months , January to May, marinating in freezing mud, ACC] to move to Vermont, but that too contributes to Vermonters' sense of community-based politics.

During my twelve years in Burlington, I went to dozens of protests and demonstrations. Some, like the People's Economic Summit in 1995 during the National Governors' Conference or the convergence against the FTAA meetings taking place in Quebec City in 2000-- were events that took months to plan and involved people from around the country. Others, like the protest against the US invasion of Iraq in 2003 and the takeover of Bernie Sanders' office during the bombing of Yugoslavia in 1999--were spontaneous and primarily involved Vermonters and college students attending college in the area. Almost all of them came off peacefully and were occasionally attended by various local politicians. Suffice it to say that Burlington is the only place that I have protested our government's actions where I never worried about getting arrested or beaten without warning. Although I always had the thought in my mind that protest in that situation was exactly what Herbert Marcuse was talking about when he wrote of repressive tolerance, I enjoyed the freedom from fear I grew to expect in Burlington.

So, imagine my surprise when I received an email from a friend still living and working in Vermont that described a new ordinance that the Burlington City Council wants to turn into law. In essence, the proposed law is an attempt to create so-called free speech zones in Burlington. Although the law doesn't state this explicitly, it does explicitly state where residents can not hold a protest: in front of the City Hall Building and in front of the office building where Bernie Sanders maintains his Burlington offices. So, by default, the ordinance does create "zones" of free speech. Furthermore, the ordinance would require 100 days advance notice for marches of 100 people or more and seven days advance notice for those of less than 100. On top of that, it would require a so-called administrative fee of fifty dollars and require groups to pay for any police protection, even if the marchers do not request such protection. Now, I don't know about you, but it seems to me that this law would not only restrict people's right to peaceably assemble and speak, it pretty much forbids that right to those unable or unwilling to pay the required fees. On top of that, the restrictions against groups gathering in front of the City Hall or the Congressperson's office contradict the very essence of a government of the people. After all, who the hell do they think built City Hall and who the hell do they think the Congressperson is working for?

Both of the aforementioned buildings are on the aforementioned Church Street. For those who have never been to Burlington, this street is essentially an open air shopping mall. Knowing the arguments of those who want to restrict the rights of those on the street who do not shop--be they politicos, street performers, teenagers looking for their friends, or homeless people--this ordinance is not a surprise. Indeed, the city attorney who drew up the measure (a so-called progressive), insists that the law is "content neutral" and just designed to permit equal access to all, shoppers and non-shoppers. The reality is the opposite. Since political protests are the primary large gatherings on the streets, it is clear to most everyone that this ordinance is intended to restrict such events. Of course, most of the folks who have lobbied the hardest for the restrictions are some of the merchants with shops on the street. The first amendment guarantees the right to peaceably assemble. It does not say we can only do this in certain areas and only after notifying the authorities. Nor does it say we should have to pay for this right. (Besides, isn't that what taxes are supposed to pay for?).

Indeed, a recent, magnificently written decision by U.S. District Court Judge John A. Woodcock, Jr in Bangor, Maine says as much. Judge Woodcock determined that an Augusta, Maine parade statue that required marchers to obtain insurance and pay other fees to the city before they could get a permit was unconstitutional. Not only did he find the ordinance unconstitutional, the judge defended the right adamantly in his 51-page opinion. He quoted previous cases that said that public streets are traditional public fora and that "the government must bear an extraordinarily heavy burden to regulate speech in such locales." (City of Richmond, 743 F.2d at 1355.32) Furthermore, wrote the judge, since "the streets are natural and proper places for the dissemination of information and opinion one is not to have the exercise of his liberty of expression in appropriate places abridged on the plea that it may be exercised in some other place". (Schneider, 308 U.S. at 163.) Nor, he continued, should there be fees associated with the right to march in city streets.

Let Representative Sanders denounce the proposed regulation in Vermont. Or does Sanders also now take the view that In the land where the dollar reigns supreme, free speech will have to pay.

In the introduction to this book, I talked about the empire of the mind. You know, that method to the advertiser's madness that somehow incorporates messages into our consciousness about the nature of freedom. An Army of one or the freedom to buy a truck that looks like everyone else's. Freedom of choice as a replacement for genuine freedom. And so on. Beyond the obvious insidiousness of advertising is the much more insistent nature of what is called culture in the modern society of capital. There is no enlightenment involved in the merchandise presented to us by car companies, banks, and other commercial failures whose primary intent is to convince us that our future involves us spending our money on their products. Indeed, there is not even a pretense or supposition that there should be any enlightenment in the equation. So, we spend our time watching and listening to these entertainment products while we work out how we'll get that new car shown to us every ten minutes during the commercial break.

Trotsky wrote that "every ruling class creates its own culture, and consequently, its own art." While one might be hard pressed to justify most television shows and most pop music as art, they are what pass for culture. Once, a conversation with a friend who worked as a college faculty member turned to the question of whether film and music reflected or created popular trends and thought. In other words, does the culture we absorb influence us or do we influence it. Naturally, there is no conclusive answer to this question and we did not reach one that day. However, there are some clear examples of each. To begin with, television shows like the quasi-fascist "24" and its less unnerving predecessors like the 007 series of films exist to instill a fear not only of the enemies of the state but of the state itself. Thusly, we are encouraged by these obviously propagandistic works to ignore or consent to whatever illegal and immoral actions taken by those who claim to protect us. Furthermore, we are subconsciously trained to identify the state's enemies as our own. Reality shows like "Cops" further this consciousness.

To substantiate the other side of the coin let me turn to the most popular rock band of all time, The Beatles. These young men arguably began as consumers who picked up musical instruments and replicated the music of their musical heroes, most of whom were bluesmen from the United States. They went on to become the most popular rock group of the

1960s and a cultural phenomenon with out parity. When the band grew their hair long and talked about LSD, were they propagandizing a new way of life or were they reflecting a way of life already in existence? To put it differently, did the Beatles and other rock bands lead the youth of the western world into the counterculture or did the counterculture consume the bands into its community? There is no clear answer to this, of course. The relationship was symbiotic at best and parasitic at its worst. Just like the later phenomenon of hip-hop, the streets created the music and the music in turn mutated, reflected and popularized the culture. Unfortunately, the aspects which were popularized were those that challenged the dominant system the least. In rock music that turned out to be the sex and drugs. In hip hop it turned out to be the sex, drugs and money. Politics and the sense of community were removed in favor of an individualistic pursuit of gratification. In other words, the capitalist ethos prevailed. This makes sense, of course, given that we live in a capitalist society and the companies that produce the music are instrumental players in that society's economy.

Even on the occasion where something truly remarkable that serves a purpose beyond titillation comes into the cultural marketplace--a phenomenon seen in cinema and music more than television--the coverage of the work and its creators is often trivialized if it is covered at all. This was brought home to me recently as I watched the coverage of the Golden Globe Awards at a friend's house. Little was said about the meaning of the films presented but thousands of words were wasted on the clothing worn by various actors and actresses as they walked around outside of the event showing off for the cameras. In the media coverage the following day, more print space was used describing people's clothing and who they were with than on the works that were nominated. When it comes to music, reviewers tend to delve a bit deeper. However, at the end of the year, it is usually the musical works that made the most money that are celebrated in the media events viewed by the general public. This usually means that the works with the least meaning are those which are publicized most. This in turn propels even more sales, leaving works of consequence to linger in the CD bins until they are dropped by the industry.

Books are quite similar. Hundreds, if not thousands of titles, are rarely acknowledged by the media, while certain authors monopolize the sales charts and the minds of the reading public. I see this phenomenon daily as a library worker. Thousands of dollars are spent buying books that read very similar to the last work by an author, while other literature is never ordered. Well-read people end up reading materials that not only endorse the thought processes of the dominant culture of consumption and alienation, but are convinced that they are consequently somehow more enlightened than those that don't read. Once again, we return to the question of which influences which. For example are second- and third-rate crime authors like Patricia Cornwell popular because people like her writing or are these authors popular because the advertising budgets behind them convince people that they should read them precisely because they are popular?

Yet, all is not lost. Even within the greater market of mainstream culture there exists artists and other creators of potentially subversive art. Most of this material requires some concerted effort to find it, but

some is as available as a Bob Dylan disc or an Alan
Moore comic.

His Satanic Majesty's Royal Knight

I saw the Rolling Stones for the first time in the autumn of 1970 in Frankfurt am Main. The show was incredible, but what I remember most vividly today is the scene outside of the place that they played-the Festhalle. As soon as concertgoers exited the streetcar, they were met with a line of police with dogs. The dogs were barking and yanking at their chains, which the cops held tightly. Various hippies stood around in small groups smoking hash and drinking wine, making drug deals, and looking for their friends.

Others, who were more politically inclined, distributed leaflets written in both German and English that decried the exploitation of rock music by big time promoters. Indeed, the price of the concert tickets was more than tickets for any other similar event. By today's standards they were still incredibly cheap (10--12 DM or about $3.50), but they were at least 3 DM higher than people were used to paying. GIs, who made up a substantial portion of every rock concert crowd in Germany, mingled with the crowd, trying their best to forget their day job.

As I made my way towards the series of entrances a small skirmish broke out between the police and a group of people who were trying to crash the gates. The next thing I knew I was being squeezed between two cops and their dogs and a group of people with no place to run. I stuck my ticket into my pants pocket and tried to squeeze past the police. Just as I found an exit I felt the bite of one of the dogs on the bottom of my pants leg. With a burst of energy propelled solely by fear, I yanked my foot loose and ran toward the entrance gate. The police were busy with the gatecrashers and did not bother to chase me. The ticket taker took my ticket, tore it, and I made my way into the concert hall.

I was in! The revolution was on and here was the soundtrack. Mick Jagger and the Rolling Stones would be on the stage at any moment. They had left riots and rebellion in their wake the last three or four years and Frankfurt was no exception. I looked once again at my torn jeans for a validation of this fact. Fortunately the dog had failed to get any flesh in its grip and only the cloth was torn. I don't remember too many of the songs the Stones played, but recall very clearly that they closed with "Street Fighting Man." At the time, this was the song in the Stones' repertoire that I wanted to hear the most. After all, it was a call to us revolutionaries-cultural and political-and it scared the establishment.

Hell, the city of Chicago had banned radio stations from playing it during the battles between police and protesters at the Democratic Convention in 1968. Armed Forces Radio never played it, perhaps from some fear that it would rile up the GIs. Of course, this wasn't the only song they had banned. The Crosby, Stills, Nash & Young song about the murders at Kent State, "Ohio," was played no more than a half dozen times before some officer ordered the radio station to stop playing it. One of the DJs (a GI) played it after the ban and was removed from his job at the station. Just like today, the military brass was extremely afraid of soldiers getting any opinions that might contradict the official one.

As those of us who had made it inside left the concert, we were met by an increased police presence in the parking lot. Apparently, the skirmishes outside had erupted into a small riot during the concert and more police had been called in to put it down. As I headed towards a streetcar stop, I reveled in the scene and thought to myself that the Stones concert was everything I expected it to be, complete with a riot outside.

The next time I saw the Stones was in 1981 at Candlestick Park in San Francisco. By this time, rock music was very big business and Mick Jagger was wearing Capri pants. His jeans and cape were gone, as were his rebellious fans. Sure, there were some fights and struggles with pushy police in the Candlestick parking lot, but no cultural revolutionaries decrying the exploitation of the culture or the $25.00 ticket price. The music was good, but the daring was gone. The Rolling Stones were mere entertainment now. Mick was a prancing rooster and the only remaining integrity left in the original group belonged to Keith Richards and Charlie Watts.

So, when I saw on the news that Mick had been knighted recently I wasn't surprised. It is a logical progression after all. There are those Stones' aficionados who have always insisted that Mick was never really the bad boy rebel he has been made out to be. Instead, say these folks, he is more like the three kings who appear in the apocryphal tale that Bob Dylan relates on the cover of his album John Wesley Harding: when asked how far they want to "go in," the first king answers, "Not too far but just far enough so's we can say that we've been there." In other words, Jagger has always been more of a poseur than the genuine article. This isn't to say the man doesn't have convictions, it just that he does not seem to have a public stance from which he can't retreat. Keith has his guitar, a bemused attitude and his rebellious core. Mick has a career.

But, you might say, Paul McCartney is a knight. My reply to that would be simply that Paul never pretended to be a rebel. He was always Paul McCartney, master songwriter and middle class guy. It was John Lennon, after all, who lobbied Paul and the other Beatles to reject their earlier medals given them by the Queen as a protest against Great Britain's support for America's war in Vietnam. You don't hear about Mick rejecting his knighthood to protest Britain's groveling support for the current US war in Iraq. Indeed, you don't hear Mick saying much of anything about the war.

Oh well, what can you expect from a culture that prostitutes itself to the highest bidder, whether it's a car manufacturer or the Super Bowl? Even overtly political rockers have to make a buck, right? This is where the contradictions take center stage. How does a political rock band make a living within the system of corporate capitalism? Jefferson Airplane released its call to revolution, Volunteers, in 1969 on the RCA label. At the time, RCA was one of the nation's top defense contractors. The Clash, who were punk rock's most radical band (and actually had a political stance beyond nihilism), recorded for Epic, owned by Sony. The revolutionary rockers of the 1990s, Rage Against the Machine, also recorded for Epic. Sony, of course, is one of the world's largest corporations and makes its money from any number of ventures, some of which are military-related. No matter what, its corporate board has little interest in the revolutionary hopes of either Tom Morello or Joe Strummer; little interest, that is, that can't be measured in dollars.

Rock bands that eschew the corporate world of the big labels may remain pure to their artistic and political beliefs but, unfortunately for their art and the art of rock itself, most of their potential audience never hears them. This, then, is the dilemma of rebel music in a world of corporate profit. Of course, Sir Mick could help out by spending some of his millions on producing some of these bands, but what would the Queen think?

Why I Love My Petty Bourgeois Tendencies

One of the reasons I was asked not to join the Revolutionary Communist Party when it was being formed in 1974-1975 was because of my petty-bourgeois tendencies. Although the RCP was quite a different animal then, I have to acknowledge that I was relieved when our cadre leader suggested that I might be more effective as a supporter instead of a member. Then, after the revolution, I joked, it would be easier to shoot me, just like the Kronstadters.

I only mention the party because one of the expressions of my petty-bourgeois tendencies was my insistence on smoking weed and going to rock concerts, especially the Grateful Dead. These practices were considered to be bourgeois decadence by many post-new left leftists. For me, they were part of what got me into the revolution in the first place. Sure, there were elements of hedonism involved in these pursuits but, like Emma Goldman is reputed to have said: "If I can't dance, I don't want to be part of your revolution."

Besides, the desire by the RCP and other such left formations to be truly "working-class" was based on a caricature of who the working class really was. Their model was the reactionary white male who carried a lunch pail to his factory job and came home at the end of the day to his beer and tract home.

There were only a few women in this working class and no young people. That wasn't the workers I knew. We slung burgers, dug basements with shovels in garden apartment building projects, painted houses and government buildings, and waited tables. Then, when the working day was over, we hit the bars where rock music played, joints were smoked, and antiwar politics and hitchhiking trips were discussed. To their credit, it didn't take long for most of those Left formations to figure out that their original perception of the working class was based on false representations that attempted to present the most reactionary workers as being the most typical.

It only took them a few years of actual participation in the workplace to realize that.

Anyhow, the only reason I'm even flashing on this is because I saw the most recent incarnation of The Dead this past weekend in Saratoga Springs, New York. This band has come and gone since the death of its inspiration and leader, Jerry Garcia, died in 1995. At first, the remaining members were not interested in reforming at all. However, as the years passed, they changed their minds and have toured under various names and with different lineups for the past two or three years.

The current lineup features the four remaining members of the Grateful Dead-Phil Lesh on bass, Bob Weir on rhythm guitar, Bill Kreutzman and Mickey Hart on percussion-Jeff Chimenti on keyboards, and Warren Haynes and Jimmy Herring on guitars. This lineup certainly comes closest to the musical spirit and abilities of the Grateful Dead (by the way, the word grateful was retired in honor of Garcia), largely because of the guitar styles of Haynes and Herring.

For those who have always considered the Dead to be just an excuse for a bunch of middle-class kids to take drugs, they miss the point. Indeed, this is certainly an element of their audience, but the same could be said about almost any rock band. In short, people don't need an excuse to get high, although rock and roll concerts certainly enhance the experience for many. The Dead have always been identified as a counterculture band. That hasn't changed. The history they represent is part of the band's appeal. Where else can people go today and feel that they are part of something that everyone knows changed the world somehow? Their audience looks considerably different than it did when I first began attending their shows, but that's to be expected-over thirty years have passed since then. The politics of the crowd-when they come up at all-tend to be more liberal than anything else, although the overwhelming sentiment is more of a gentle libertarianism of the mutual aid type. Not in the negative sense, but in a "leave me alone and let me have my own life" sense. The more popular political tables at their shows tend to be those representing environmental and peace organizations. Overall, though, the show and surrounding scene is mostly about having a good peaceful time.

On to the music. The show I saw started off slowly. The band struggled to find its groove through most of the first set, finally pulling it together on the last song "The Music Never Stopped." This song is a celebration of the potential power that music has. You know, when it takes you away from the heat and the worry and transports you to this place where everybody's dancing and smiling. The version this night was a frolic that had echoes of calypso with a rock and roll backbeat. Weir's voice fit in nicely with the guitars and bass as the song spiraled to its chorus and back down. Then silence.

It was the second set when the music truly kicked in. August 1st is Jerry Garcia's birthday and his spirit was apparent in the selections played. Almost every song was a tribute to the spirit and legacy of the counterculture's inspirations and mentors. The highlight was Rev. Gary Davis' blues classic "Death Don't Have No Mercy." Warren Haynes' guitar soared above the crowd, retrieving Garcia's soul and sowing it among the dancing fans. This was the blues in its transcendent form-telling us all about death and its permanence in the human experience, but making that somehow okay, as if we were some Zen master and not afraid of it at all. It wasn't just Garcia's spirit coming through Warren Haynes' guitar; it was Willie Dixon's, John Lee Hooker's, Robert Johnson's, Muddy Waters', Son House, Jimi Hendrix's, and the spirit of every guitarist who ever played the blues he or she knew in their gut and soul. Mourning as ecstasy. (Of course, I couldn't help thinking of Iraq, where death truly has no mercy).

Next came Garcia's paean to the dead songstress, Janis Joplin, "Birdsong." Lesh did a fair job of singing this beautiful poem to the lady of the Haight and, by doing so, turned it into a tribute to Jerry as well.

Anyone who sings a tune so sweet is passin' by,
Laugh in the sunshine, sing, cry in the dark, fly
through the night.
Don't cry now, don't you cry, don't you cry
anymore.
Sleep in the stars, don't you cry, dry your eyes on
the wind

From there, the band rambled into a Robert Hunter take on the old tale of love and lying titled "Ruben and Cherisse." Then came a rather ethereal, spacey percussion jam with various keyboards and electric guitar sounds intermingled in-kind of like Sun Ra when he goes beyond the astral plane and onto that plane for which there is no name. This slowly and slyly slipped into the Dead's take on Pink Floyd's paean to its founder and genius, Syd Barrett: "Shine On You Crazy Diamond." Similarly, the Dead sang this to Garcia. Once again, Haynes took the piece and moved it up into the stratosphere. This time, he had plenty of help from Jimmy Herring, a subtly accomplished guitarist whose jazz-like licks complemented the serious electric blues that emanate from Haynes ax. From there, we were treated to a raucous and rocking version of the Dead tune "St. Stephen"-a rather arcane tale by Robert Hunter (Dead lyricist) about some prophet who may or may not have existed in the Haight in 1967 or in some

Brueghel village in the Middle Ages. Like many of Hunter's works, you feel like the tale he is telling is older than language itself yet as new as the trip you took last week. This song is a cautionary tale about trusting those who would allow themselves to be made into prophets that is set to a tune that motivates even the dead to dance. Finishing up with their quick history course on the origins of the counterculture San Francisco-style, "The Other One," the Dead kept the crowd on their feet with their arms and bodies flailing and sneakily slipped into "Goin' Down the Road Feelin' Bad," rendered this time with a sparse guitar accompaniment and tuneful harmonies. Then, as if bidding Garcia's spirit goodbye and releasing it back into the skies full of stars above us, they continued their harmonies with an accapella rendition of the bluegrass gospel tune "The Angel Band."

As the crowd filtered into the night, I moved with them, ready for another round of life's daily grind and all the stupidity and commercialized consciousness I would encounter.

ZAP Comics Redux

I've always been something of a comic book fan.
Captain Marvel, Batman, Green Lantern, even Richie
Rich and Archie. When I was 10 years old and was
evacuated from the small military base I lived on in
Peshawar, West Pakistan because of a war between
India and Pakistan over Kashmir, the thing I remember
the best is the incredible number of comic books at the
disposal of all the youngsters I was evacuated with. We
spent hours reading comics that other military
dependents and GIs had donated to us. When our plane
stopped over in Tehran for a refueling on its way from
Kabul, Afghanistan to Istanbul, Turkey the Red Cross
and USO volunteers gave us each a bag lunch and three
comics. Mine were two Supermans and a very old
Captain Marvel. I don't remember the contents of the
lunch at all. The first few days in Turkey, all of the boys
over six years old slept in a barracks dorm on
Karamursel Air Station. There were several hundred
comic books strewn around the place. Unfortunately, we
eventually had to go back to school and my comic
reading time was cut short. Although I still read them
when I could, my obsessive binge was curtailed.

I regained some of that obsession the day I saw the first three ZAP Comix in a head shop in Germany. For those of you unfamiliar with ZAPs, they were the best of the underground comix that were published in the late 1960s and throughout the 1970s. R. Crumb, Denis Kitchen, Spain, S. Clay Wilson, Moscosco, Robert Williams and so on-all of the best artists filled the pages of these psychedelic, mind-bending, rude and anti-establishment exercises in expression. Part of the rebellion against the moralistic Comics Code that mainstream comics had to adhere to, underground comix laughed in the face of this attempt by the puritans to regulate what people could read. If someone was looking for a way to be offended, they could find it in ZAP. For the rest of us, ZAPs and their sister publications were cutting social and political criticism. Whether it was R. Crumb drawing and writing a story about Whiteman, the screwed-up representative of male middle-class America or S. Clay Wilson sharing his intricately drawn tales of brutality and excess among bikers and pirates, these comix rearranged the often-dull world we live in. They weren't light reading and sometimes not very pretty, but neither is the daily news. At least comix are fun.

GIs loved Dopin' Dan, a hapless GI who fumbled his way through the man's army stoned on weed and whatever else was around. A Beetle Bailey for the Vietnam generation of soldiers, Dan's primary concern was staying alive, staying high, and making a fool of the lifers who tried to rule his world. Gilbert Shelton from Austin had his tales of the Fabulous Furry Freak Brothers, three twenty something men who had dropped out of Middle America and moved to the hippie ghettos. Their bumbling adventures avoiding cops, the draft, and work were not only humorous, they were what we were living. ZAP Comix combined such underground comix characters as Mr. Natural and Coochie-Cootie, The Checkered Demon and Trashman, Agent of the 6th International. The latter was an anarcho-syndicalist superhero created out of the cartoonist Spain's interest in politics and the anarchists of the Spanish Civil War. Often quite sexist in their portrayal of women, these comix reflected the society they existed in. The sexism did not go unanswered, however. Several women cartoonists began a series of comix they titled All-Wimmin Comix that saw the new world of the counterculture from a feminist perspective. Like much good satire, these comix used exaggeration to make their point. It was this exaggeration (that bordered on the grotesque at times) that got them in trouble with prudes of the right and the left.

I recently purchased the most recent issue of ZAP-Number 15. Like its predecessors, there is something to offend anyone who wishes to be offended here. Heck, parts of it offend me. Is it for children, like other comics supposedly are? If your definition of children means those younger than high school age, my answer would be no, at least in most cases. Ken Kesey (an avid Captain Marvel fan) once noted in a published conversation with Paul Krassner that when his kids read underground comix, their style of play "turned inward." Kesey attributed this in part to the cartoonists' tendency to use their art as a way to work out some of their demons. Adults, argued Kesey, either had enough of their own demons to deal with or had built enough walls that enabled them not to take on someone else's. Children, on the other hand, don't have such walls. Despite this, I would rather see a ZAP comic in the hands of a child than support a call to limit their sales or censor their content.

Content-wise, ZAP 15 takes on the new police state of the post 9-11 America. While satirizing US residents' fear of terrorists, Shelton, Crumb and the other artists in the collection take on the puritanical persuasions of the current administration and its manipulation of fear to create the police state it desires. Whether it's R. Crumb's autobiographical sketch of his neuroses, Spain's portrayal of the car-racing culture, S. Clay Wilson's grotesque artistry portraying the underside of human existence in no uncertain terms, or Gilbert Shelton's latest Wonder Warthog adventure where in the Warthog's alter-ego Hebert Desenex loses his job and his superpowers (gee what could that mean?) and then gets arrested for looking like a terrorist just because he's weird, ZAP 15 continues the grand underground tradition of getting under that bit of the Establishment's skin we all wear. . Despite the intention of satire (it is a comic after all), there are elements of this comic that are more real than fantasy, more truth than fiction. Than again, isn't that the nature of satire? To take the facts and make them so real (super real, in fact) that the truth comes through? Jonathan Swift did it back when he wrote "A Modest Proposal," and the aforementioned Paul Krassner made a publishing career out of it with his now-defunct magazine, The Realist. In other words, many a good satirist adopts the philosophy of "screw 'em if they can't take a joke." ZAP and its artists continue this tradition.

The Last Poets Recalled

Summer 1971. Frankfurt am Main, Germany. I was hanging out with a friend in his room in the Westend section of the city. We were reading Zap Comix and some new underground papers he had brought back with him from the States. A bowl of hashish had set us up nice and the Grateful Dead's Anthem of the Sun was spinning on his turntable. The music was turned low so as not to disturb his neighbors on the other side of the paper-thin wall of the rooming house. The two men who lived there, one from some place in western Africa and the other a Black man recently discharged from the US Army, worked nights and needed their sleep. Just when Pigpen began the song "Alligator" on the Dead album, a loud, intense percussive beat came through the wall. My first thought was that one of the neighbors was playing a conga. Then came the chanting voices "When the revolution comes/some of us will catch it on TV/with chicken hanging from our mouths/you'll know it's revolution/because there won't be no commercials/when the revolution comes." My friend nodded. "It's The Last Poets again."

I had met the neighbors once before when they were selling the local Black Panther paper, *Voice of the Lumpen*. So, on my way out of the building I stopped at their room to say hello and inquire about the music I had just heard. The vet suggested I borrow the album to give it a better listen. I did. Six months later it was for sale in the base Post Exchange and I bought it. Soon thereafter, the Poets second album, This Is Madness, was available in the German record stores downtown. This album included their classic, "The White Man's Got a God Complex." Later that spring, some African-American friends of mine formed a music group that performed songs by the Last Poets and Rahsaan Roland Kirk. The only times I saw them perform were at a Black Student Union assembly in our high school and at a concert at Goethe Universitat in Frankfurt, where they opened for the German rock band GURU GURU.

The Last Poets formed on May 19, 1968-Malcolm X's birthday. They borrowed their name from a line in a poem by South African poet Willie Kgositsile that goes:

> When the moment hatches in time's womb there will be no art talk,
> The only poem you will hear will be the spearpoint pivoted in the punctured marrow of the villain....

Therefore we are the last poets of the world.

Driven by the steady rhythm of the percussion instruments they played, this assemblage of artists chanted songs about life in the urban streets of black America and challenged its inhabitants to get off their butts and do something about it. Their masterpiece poem, "Niggers are Scared of Revolution," portrays a population that was looking for ways to be bought off by the corporate world as hard as those who populated its white counterpart. In a graphic description of Black America's version of the one-dimensional nightmare described by Herbert Marcuse that we all live in, the Last Poets satirized the susceptibility of their listeners to Madison Avenue's latest scam. In their case, it was the "Black is Beautiful" marketing then beginning to take over the world that African-Americans lived in. In the counter-culture's case, it was the commodification of everything from the music to the drugs and even to the politics. By 1970, the Poets had released their first album. Not until hip-hop came along would the world hear something like their sound again.

Primarily geared toward an African-American audience, the song poems on the record talked about life in the Black enclaves of the US. In a vein first explored by poet Langston Hughes, Omar Ban Hassen, Alafia Pudim, and Abiodun Oyewole pound out verses about riding the New York subway up to Harlem, making love and hanging out in Black America in the middle of the 20th century. Like Hughes, there is beauty and blemish, hope and hopelessness, and life and death in their rhymes. Interspersed among these vignettes of African-American street culture are calls for Blacks in the US to rise up against the white establishment and mockeries of this audience's refusal to throw out the system that has oppressed them for so long. Oyewole would be convicted of robbery soon after the album's appearance on the US album charts. He was sentenced to fourteen years and did four.

If I were to classify the politics of the Last Poets, I would place them in the same general sphere as the part of the Internationalist wing of the Black Panther Party that became the Black Liberation Army. This wing, which was nominally led by Eldridge Cleaver from his exile in Algeria, was best represented by the New York chapter of the Party. More nationalist than Marxist-Leninist, this philosophy held with the Panther argument that the only true African-American nationalism was a nationalism that understood that the economic oppression experienced by blacks in the United States was fundamental to their national identity. However, unlike the Panthers, the Last Poets were more separatist than the international wing or the wing led by the Oakland, CA. chapter. Other forms of Black nationalism, like that promoted by United Slaves leader Ron Karenga and others, ignored the economic oppression of African-Americans and focused more on the Black nation's African roots. In the language of the Panthers and their supporters, this was considered to be reactionary nationalism, as opposed to the revolutionary nationalism of the Panthers.

It was this reactionary nationalism that enabled the African-American struggle for liberation to be manipulated by the very marketplace that oppressed them. Without an understanding of the role that US capitalism played in their oppression, Black people in the US were led to believe that could express their identity by wearing dashikis, buying Jet magazine and using Afro-Sheen cosmetic products. In a manner quite similar to the marketplace's cooptation of the counterculture revolution among the young white citizens of the US, the ability of capitalism to co-opt the trappings of the Black liberation movement was spelling that revolution's death, too. Of course, the willingness of the adherents of these liberation movements to go along with the manipulations of the market made this process all the simpler. This bit from the Last Poets' song "Niggers Are Scared of Revolution," makes this case quite clearly:

> Niggers always going through bullshit changes.
> But when it comes for a real change
> Niggers are scared of revolution.

The Last Poets' second album, *This Is Madness,* explores the themes of the first album even further. One difference, however, is a more explicit anger towards not only the system but towards the average white person who upholds that system. Unlike the first album, the Poets focus some of their rage on the ordinary white men and women who support the system, actively or tacitly. In other words, those of us who live within the dynamic of white privilege and do nothing to fight that dynamic. Conversely, other songs here are considerably more positive in their estimation of blacks than the songs on the first release. If the first album was the late 1960s version of Langston Hughes, then this album is the early 1970s version of Amiri Baraka-anger that is ready to explode at any time and at anyone who might even look like the enemy. In short, this album is representative of the time: cops and Feds killing and jailing radicals, Blacks and hippies; racists and reactionaries calling for a police state with Nixon and company happy to oblige; and revolutionaries blowing up buildings and attacking cops. Tolerance was not a word taken to heart by many because too many people felt that the time had passed for that sentiment.

In a song whose title is more figurative than literal (if only because the white man's also got some darker-skinned folks doing his dirty work), the Last Poets provide the listener with a succinct analysis of European-American imperialism. Titled "The White Man's Got A God Complex," this piece lays out the fundamental motivation for the mess of a world that colonialism and imperialism has made. It could easily have been written today. On the top of a syncopated rhythm that mixes the mood of the street with that of the African-American Sunday church service (and a little Howlin' Wolf thrown in), this poem's last verse provides the listener with their ten-line outline of the world's history ever since Columbus hit Hispaniola.

> A'makin' guns. I'm God!
> A'makin' bombs. I'm God!
> A'makin' gas. I'm God!

....
Killed Indians who discovered him. I'm God!
Killed Japanese with the A-bomb. I'm God!
Killed and still killin' black people. I'm God!
Enslaving the earth. I'm God!
Done went to the moon. I'm God!

Add a line or two (How about, Killed some Arabs and more Africans. I'm God! Put Bayview on the TV screens of the world. I'm God!) and the song works all too well for today, which may be why they still occasionally perform. George Bush and Bill Clinton still wouldn't get it, but the Last Poets weren't writing for them, anyhow.

Trying in Vain to Breathe the Fire We Was Born In

Two of my friends had finally scored. They had been standing outside of the Carter Barron Theater in Washington, DC every evening during that July week in 1975 hoping to find somebody willing to let go of a couple tickets to see Bruce Springsteen and the E Street Band. It had taken them all week, but they had managed to find tickets to the last show. I had purchased mine weeks earlier after standing in line for most of a night.

Bruce and his band weren't yet the larger-than-life phenomenon they were to eventually become. Indeed, he could still claim to be the working stiff's rocker. His lyrics while always convincing were still being drawn from the band's common experiences. These were experiences they shred with their (then) mostly East Coast audiences. The local FM radio station in DC had been playing the single "Born to Run" from the group's forthcoming album as often as they could all summer. In addition, the station had obtained some acetates of a couple other tunes from the album of the same name and were playing the shit out of them, too. Bruce was about to break loose. He was going national.

That was all unimportant, though. What was
important was the music and the words. Springsteen's
lyrics weren't transcendent or decadent. Unlike the
Grateful Dead's *Workingman's Dead* or The Band's
repertoire, his songs weren't about a land that harkened
back to the days of the pioneers. Nor did they tell of an
ideal Woodstock Nation like that found in Crosby, Stills,
Nash & Young's *Deja Vu* and the rest of the Dead's
songbook. They certainly weren't frivolous like the disco
then hustling its way onto the national dance floor nor
pseudo-surreal like the progressive rock of Pink Floyd
or Yes. No, Bruce sang about lives lived where one knew
that when s/he grew up s/he was going to go to work at
some shit job just to pay the bills. Either that, or end up
in jail trying to avoid such a life.

Still, there was a tinge of hope in the songs on *Born
To Run*. This hope is implicit in the title song. "Baby
this town rips the bones from your back,it roars, It's a
death trap, it's a suicide rap, We gotta get out while
we're young `Cause tramps like us, baby we were born
to run." Climb in your car, find a lover, and get on the
road. That was the answer. Of course, as the song
continues, we discover that "There's no place left to
hide." This means, of course, that we probably never

will get out of the death trap that our destiny has set for us and the best we can do is just run, even if there's no place to go.

If one recalls, 1975 was the year that the US military lost in Vietnam. The president was Gerald Ford, who was there because he promised to pardon the previous occupier of the White House for all crimes he might have been convicted of. The lie had been exposed for the cheap charade that it was. There was no morality at the top. Even the government's supporters were admitting what was so obvious to the rest of us. This country was run by a bunch of self-serving crooks that would stop at nothing to keep their power. If this was the case, then what was wrong with running your own hustle, especially if it's for love? This is exactly the scenario in "Meeting Across the River." A pair of young wannabe gangsters is hoping to finally make the big score, but only if they don't screw up like they usually do. Of course, if they screwed up, they would have to answer for it, unlike the guys at the top. Everything on this album is ultimately for love. This is the one true salvation in a world where nothing is as it seems. So jump in.

Such is not the case on Springsteen's other master work, *Born In the USA*. Love has run its course by the time this album is through. Desolation and despair are the just as likely results of adolescent hopes and infatuations. Growing older has only made life more desperate. Running has only brought us to an abyss even greater than those we faced back in our years fresh out of high school when the world was falling apart but our lives were still fresh. From the burned-out and bitter Vietnam veteran whose song opens the album to the working class hard luck cases in the songs "Working On the Highway"and "Downbound Train," running has only brought them closer to the end. There is no hope at the end of the trail, only more running and the back seat of a black-and-white.

Despite the overriding despair, some of the songs still ache for even a trace of hope. Hope in the simple things, like refusing to surrender or something as seemingly silly as changing ones looks. Any hope one finds, however, is based on the slimmest of premises in a world of shadows and lies a world made even more false in the fake morning light of Ronald Reagan's presidency. *Born In the USA* (the album and the song) spell out the shallowness and hypocrisy of 1980s

America, whether its in the dead-end life of a veteran of Americas war on the Vietnamese or the dead-end lives of young guys from Manhattan heading to Jersey for the Fourth of July (with one of them ending up handcuffed to the bumper of a state trooper's Ford.) In an ironic twist, Mr. Reagan actually used the song "Born In the USA" as a backdrop to a couple of his re-election campaign rallies in New Jersey before Springsteen demanded that he stop. While its not surprising that Reagan's workers didn't understand the nuances of the song, the fact of its brief appearance in the Reagan campaign belies that campaign's very shallowness. (In a similar show of right-wingers not "getting" this song, a group of pro-war students here in Burlington, VT blared the chorus this past winter from their car stereo in a vain attempt to drown out an antiwar rally.)

The last time I saw Springsteen and the E Street band in concert was in September 1985. He was playing a two-night stand in Oakland Coliseum. I had obtained a ticket through pure luck: some friends had found one on the ground as they walked through the Coliseum parking lot from the BART train stop. I happened to cross paths with them and they handed me the ducat. The show rocked from beginning to end. Towards the end of the second set, Springsteen introduced the Woody Guthrie song "This Land Is Your Land" with a request that we leave a couple bucks with the folks in the lobby who were collecting money for the homeless shelters and food banks that were springing up like mushrooms after a rain in Mr. Reagan's America. Then he told the audience which United States it was that Woody had been writing about when he wrote that tune. In so many words, it wasn't the America that Mr. Reagan was working for. It is, however, an America that is always there, even in the darkest of times.

The Music of Big Bill Broonzy

Back in the early 1970s I worked at an International House of Pancakes in a suburban Maryland town. The pay was lousy, the work was hot and rapid-fire, and my fellow workers were all pretty cool. There was one in particular who sticks out in my mind. He was the manager (not that that means anything in the food service business except that one works more hours for not much more pay than the folks (s)he supervises)-a forty year old Black man from Kansas City who had done a little time in prison and a lot of time in the streets. His wit was remarkably cutting at times. Other times it was full of warmth and humanity. The thing I liked best were his stories and his singing. The man was a treasury of tunes, especially old blues and R and B.

We both worked a shift every Friday and Saturday night that kept us in the kitchen from 6 in the evening until 6 the following morning. Fortunately, I had a friend who was a pharmacist's assistant. She managed to save a couple pills out of every shipment of speed and was more than happy to share them with my co-worker and me. It was after these pills kicked in on these evenings when the songs began to roll. They might include the Coasters "Charlie Brown" to "They all ask for me, The cows ask, the pigs ask, they all ask for me." I was working with a human jukebox. My favorite of his songs was a blues that the late Big Bill Broonzy wrote called "Black, Brown and White." When my boss got to singing this song, he had every cracker in the restaurant looking towards the kitchen. It always seemed to me that they were afraid that their just desserts were coming out the kitchen door any minute. It was all just a little speed-fueled fun, but the white folks didn't know that.

Big Bill Broonzy was born in Mississippi in late June of 1893. Soon afterwards his family moved to Arkansas. He lived the life of a poor black in America's south. One of seventeen children, he began work in the fields early and was sharecropping by 1915. However, when the drought ruined the harvest a year later, he went off to work in the mines and in 1917 he was called into the Army. When he came back home he was restless and bored. He got a job on the trains and headed to Chicago where he picked up guitar playing. By the 1930s he was making records on small "race record" recording labels. Like so many other folk-blues musicians of his time, it was John Hammond who brought Broonzy to a larger audience. This occurred when he performed at a Carnegie Hall concert in 1939 titled "Spirituals to Swing." Even with the greater commercial success Big Bill experienced in the wake of his wider audience, he was never wealthy. Like so many other African-Americans of his time, most of the money never reached his pockets.

Although Broonzy and others in his genre were often called to play spirituals, he considered himself a blues musician through and through. When asked why, he would tell a story about a turtle he caught to eat. After his uncle chopped off the turtle's head, the turtle walked headless back to the stream where Bill had caught it. As Bill told the story, his uncle told him "There's a turtle who's dead and don't know it." Big Bill would continue: "And that's the way a lot of people is today: they got the blues and they don't know it." According to his autobiography, Big Bill Blues, he first played a fiddle he made out of a cigar box when he was ten. It was after he moved to Chicago and worked as a Pullman porter that he learned guitar.

Much of Big Bill's repertoire is the standard stuff that blues are made of. You know--women doing him wrong or spending all his money and women spending

227

all his money and then doing him wrong. Other songs in his pocket are full of sexual innuendo and bravado. Still others are a variation of the blues lament. My favorite from this group has a verse that goes like this: "The men in the mine baby/They all lookin' down at me/Gal I'm down so low baby/I'm low as I can be/Yeah now baby/Girl I'm down as I can be/Gal I'm down so low baby/Ooh Lord everybody's lookin' down on poor me." All of this, of course, sung to the melodic guitar play backed up with a percussive thumb stroke on those lower strings.

Broonzy's songs weren't all women, whiskey and personally caused hard luck, though. Some of his best songs dealt with tragedy and injustice. These excerpts from his 1937 "Southern Flood Blues" evoke a fear and sense of loss that every person who's been the victim of natural disaster can feel to their bones:

I was hollerin' for mercy, and it weren't no boats around
Hey I was hollerin' for mercy, and it weren't no boats around...
Hey that looks like people, I've gotta stay right here and drown
It was dark as midnight, people began to holler and scream

Listen to this piece and you're on the roof of your house going down a river whose rage is relentless-a rage with little hope of being soothed. This same sense of rage seethes just underneath the surface of my two favorite Broonzy songs, barely keeping the volcanic ash of his anger from raining down on the listener: "I Wonder When I'll Get To Be Called A Man," and "Black, Brown And White." These are songs about the most despairing blues of all. Those are the blues that don't have to be. Blues that exist not because of a misunderstanding in love or a poor crop or even a terrible flood, but because of ignorance and fear and the hatred that combination spawns.

The first song asks the question at the end of every verse: "I wonder when I'll get to be a man?" Big Bill asks the listener (and the system that keeps his people down) what does it take? He's been in the man's military and fought for them overseas, he's worked on the levee and chopped down their trees. He's played all their games and he's gone to school. "When," he wonders. "when will I get to be called a man/Do I have to wait till I get ninety-three?" The second song, "Black, Brown and White," was the song my co-worker used to sing. Like "I Wonder When I'll Get to Be Called a Man," the song is a litany of injustices done to African-Americans in the US solely because they aren't white. From the verse about a bar where he was refused service to the verse about his trouble finding a job, this song leaves no doubt about how the system sees him. The title's reference to brown is a not-so-subtle dig at the gradations of prejudice based on how dark one actually is. In other words, the darker one's skin is, the less chances this country provides. I think Big Bill sums it up in the final verse and chorus:

> I helped win sweet victory
> With my plough and hoe
> Now I want you to tell me brother
> What you gonna do about the old Jim Crow?
> Now if you was white, should be all right
> If you was brown, could stick around
> But if you black, whoa brother, git back git back git back.

These aren't sentiments of submission. They are insightful and acerbic criticisms of the society in which Big Bill lived. It is a society in which these criticisms are truer than they should be at this juncture in our history.

Singers In a Dangerous Time

Menacingly. That's how the rock band played Saturday night. Warnings, war, and apocalypse. Two riders did approach. The wind began to howl. Electric guitars sliced the night. The singer's voice made their sword double-edged. The songs of heartbreak and the workingman's plight sung by the singer before seemed almost lighthearted in comparison. Okie From Muskogee was sung tongue-in-cheek although some in the audience still took the lyrics at the 1969 best.

Yep. Bob Dylan and Merle Haggard pulled into town Saturday night. The guy playing sax in the street out front of the civic center put it this way: These guys are giants and their tag-teaming y'all. Enjoy the show. Then he blew a nice version of "Somewhere over the Rainbow." I found a couple to buy the extra tickets I ended up with and went inside. There was a good mix of people. Young, old, a couple fellows with confederate flags on their t-shirts (it is the South, not that that makes much difference), a few guys in overalls, lots of young men and women with the requisite cellphone hung on their belt or in their hand, a few African-Americans, and mostly women and men in the middle of their lifespans.

At exactly 8:00, the Strangers took the stage, sans Merle Haggard. One of the musicians said hello and the band kicked into some warm up music. After the second song--Waylon Jennings' "I've Always Been Crazy (But It Kept Me From Going Insane)," he left the lead mike and took his place among the rest of the band. From the side of the stage, a grizzled man strode out, all in black with a cowboy hat. Merle Haggard, my friends. His set included some gems like "Mama Tried" and "Silver Wings." For those unfamiliar with Haggard's repertoire, the first is a classic country blues sung by a fellow who "turned 21 in prison/doin' life without parole." He's not seeking to blame anyone for his misfortune, thought because, after all, mama "tried to raise him better" but he ignored them all. That's a strain one hears in Haggard's tunes. Essentially libertarian, he rarely places blame for personal misfortune on others. Even when Haggard sings and writes about those who spend their lives growing up in migrant labor camps, it's a tale of family woe.

When he longs for a past America, he is longing for the freedoms that men had back then, not for its wars or social, sexual and racial prejudices. That's why he has spoken out against the Bush government and its wars and repression. As for that song "Okie From Muskogee," it's just a joke to Merle these days, despite the fact that some folks on both sides of that Sixties divide still fail to see the irony of singing it in 2006.

Musically, the Strangers were tighter than a piece of sundried rawhide. Although my violin-playing friend sitting next to me kept saying how Haggard could have done with five or six players instead of the nine he had onstage, the fact that he had horns and a saxophone player when his arrangement called for one did complete the sound. The fiddle player played with a classical control and a fiddler's abandon. The pedal steel player used sparing licks and subtle dynamics, while the keyboard player plinked out honkytonk runs straight out of that bar band I used to see in suburban Washington, DC back in the 1970s. Indeed, I felt as if I were transported to that dive whose primary habitués were washed out beehive blondes and retired truckdrivers. As if to make my vision complete, Merle and the Strangers ended the show with a hoedown on "If You Got the Money Honey, I Got the Time," turning the arena floor into a giant dance floor.

Darkness at the break of noon. Menacing anger. Snarls of refusal. Electric guitar riffs tearing through my skull and into my chest. Dylan began his set with "Maggie's Farm." Maggie's Farm where the National Guard stands around your door. And everybody wants you to be just like them. Standing at his keyboard, Dylan sneered his way through the song, holding on to the hard rock style that seems to fit this song the best. Raw and emotional rejection of the way things have become. That's the essence of this song. Ripping off the veneer of complacency and challenging himself and the audience to go beyond just being bored. It's not a question of whether or not one can afford not to work on Maggie's Farm no more. It's a question of whether one can.

The set wasn't all anger. Love songs were sung and celebrations of summer days. Yet the most powerful tunes this evening were the ones that called this world of war , torture, lies and greed into question. The songs came one after the other, giving the audience little time to breathe. When the first notes of "Blind Willie McTell" came through the air, Dylan the bluesman took the stage. It's not that he was channeling Charley Patton or the aforementioned McTell as much as he was channeling the lives of those for whom the blues were made. The downtrodden. The huddled masses. The poor immigrant. Those who toil in a land where "power and greed and corruptible seed/seem to be all that there is." Maybe there really is some truth to that arrow on the doorpost telling us this land is condemned.

That's what that darkness at the break of noon is all about. I've heard Dylan perform this song several times, but I've never heard it like I did this time. From the moment those first words left his mouth, there was a sense that someone was calling in from the Mojave desert. Dylan the prophet was here for a song's worth of time. The band played this tune as if it were stuck on a railroad crossing on Highway 61 with trains hurtling toward their vehicle from both sides. Angry at their situation and resigned to its denouement. And theirs. The menace is in in the daily hypocrisies of life and the lies of the President of the United States as he tries to start the next world war.

War that benefits the target of his song "Masters of War." One gets the idea that Dylan would like to retire this song but those masters just won't let him. There is no way to sing this song without anger. Indeed, it's probably Dylan's angriest song. It's certainly the only one that offers its targets no possibility of redemption. The only answer to what these people have done to their planet and the people who pay the price of their deeds is death. Dylan's performance of this song in Asheville made it clear that his opinion on this matter has not changed. I know that I would stand on the graves of Rumsfeld and Cheney to make sure that they are dead. Too many think that life is but a joke. Dylan makes it clear that it's not to be trifled with. The last time I saw Dylan was in New York a few weeks after the tragedies of 9-11. His band was slightly different and his tone was, too. Resignation and even some uncertainty. This time there was little of that.

Neither Haggard or Dylan are without their contradictions. That's the nature of their shared humanity. It's how they laugh at those contradictions that provides some of the appeal they have to their audience. When Merle sings "I think I'll just sit here and drink," it's more than a man crying in his beer. It's also a man that understands that life provides us with alternatives to heartbreak and woe, as well. When Dylan laughs at his misfortune in affairs of the heart, singing "You just pick anyone, An' pretend that you never have met," he's laughing at the charade that love can sometimes be. Indeed, the songs of both men can help us laugh at the charade that life itself sometimes is. If not that, their music lightens the load.

May Day 2006 in Asheville, North Carolina

May Day in North Carolina, USA. The weather is perfect. A march for immigrant rights begins this afternoon--part of the nationwide movement to prevent the passage of a legislation that would make it a felony offense to be in the US without papers or to help anyone that is here without said papers. As an organizing pamphlet stated: "Not since the Fugitive Slave Law of the 1800s has there been such a piece of repressive legislation passed in the US."

Like the aforementioned Fugitive Slave Act, HR 4437 would make it a felony to help out a fellow human being trying to make a better life for themselves and their family. The point of the protests and the May Day 2006 boycott was to prevent that legislation, which is known as HR 4437 in the House. After that point of agreement, the demands diverge.

I've been helping a friend homeschool her eleven-year-old daughter this semester. The May Day protest in Asheville was her week's lesson in real democracy. There are two things that make a democracy, she told me as we walked from our house to the Catholic church in downtown Asheville where the opening rally was taking place when we arrived. The first is protesting for change and the second is voting. Tuesday will be this week's second lesson in democracy, then. That's when North Carolina holds its primary elections. I hope that the Congressman from my district will end up with an opponent in November that can beat him. So did most of the people present at the rally, since Congressman Taylor voted for HR 4437.

When we arrived at the church, the speakers were already talking. The primary content of the speeches was liberal in nature, but the signs and banners varied from slogans echoing the philosophy summed up best by the words "No One is Illegal" to signs stating (in Spanish and English) "Nos somos Americanos."

Besides the speeches, there were also detailed legal instructions announced repeatedly over the loudspeakers and distributed in leaflet form throughout the crowd. These instructions were necessary given the uncertain immigration status of some of the participants. They included phone numbers for legal aid should any of the participants face reprisals in the future because of their participation in the protest.

One of the speakers asked how many of the rallygoers had skipped work or school. When the question was asked in English the response was loud.

When the question was asked in Spanish, the response was deafening. There weren't that many speeches, since every phrase had to be translated, either from English to Spanish or from Spanish to English.

The march began. It was orderly and it was loud. Most of the bystanders, no matter what their skin tone, honked their car horn or gave another sign of agreement. Those who disagreed either said nothing or cursed quietly to their friends. Oh, yeah, there was one guy that held a sign calling on "Real Americans" to take back their country. People on the march ignored him. Pointedly. Before the entire group of marchers had passed him by, he had left. Slogans shouted by the marchers varied from "Si Se Puede" to "El Pueblo Unido jamas sera vencido" to the variation on the latter-"Latinos Unido jamas sera vencido."

As the march progressed hundreds more joined. Most of them were Latinos that had finally made it downtown. Police were generally pleasant, although there were some with cameras on parking garage rooftops using telephoto lenses to take pictures of the march participants. If those photos end up in the hands of the INS, I won't be surprised.

A band greeted us when we arrived at the end of the march. When they finished their tune, each member was introduced with their family's heritage included. The point was obviously to remind the crowd and the media that most of us are either immigrants or descendants of immigrants. In the part of the country where the Cherokee Trail of Tears began, this should not be big news. Yet every time a new group of immigrants wants their place at the US table, it seems like the entire country needs to be reminded of our real history. The good and the bad.

My homeschool charge and I left the ending rally after another song by the band. One thing I noticed as we walked to the bus stop was that downtown Asheville, which is usually quite slender on Latino faces and the Spanish language, was full of Latinos this evening. I don't know what the La Dia Sin Immigrantes looked like in other parts of the United States, but here in Asheville, NC it was a day of witness for those of us who really believe that no human is illegal.

The Post-Racial American Myth

When I got on the bus last April (2008) after
Barack Obama's primary victory in North Carolina, the
conversation was, naturally enough, about that victory.
Despite its southern location, the town I live in —
Asheville, NC — is known for its liberal politics and
social tolerance. Consequently, the overriding tone was
one of exuberance. Young black men and older veterans
of the desegregation struggles of the 1960s smiled
knowingly at each other. Indeed, one fellow said to
every black person who got on the bus — "Black
President." Occasionally, he gave the new passenger
what the right wing called a "terrorist fist pump." If
there was somebody on the bus who objected to this
display, they kept their mouth shut. Yet, beyond this
show is the simmering hatred of that element of the US
polity which resents the fact that a black man is the
president. This group will use any motivation to
prevent Obama from any success while simultaneously
dragging him to the right because of his fear of this
essentially fascist element. They hide their hatred
behind a concern for the constitution which, when you
think about that document historically, is not that far

off the mark given its genesis at the hands of slaveowners and other men of property.

I was out in Oakland, CA. recently for a friend's birthday (January 2009). Naturally, I visited Telegraph Ave. in Berkeley–my old stomping grounds–while I was there. Things have changed there while remaining the same. The area is certainly much more ethnically diverse. Gentrification has slithered in, but its presence is quite minimal when compared to other sections of Berkeley, Oakland or San Francisco. Peoples Park looks better than it has in years, with its native plant life dominating the east and west ends of that small piece of turf where so many battles have been fought. Doorways that used to shelter street people have been blocked off and some benches have been removed from areas where those same folks used to relax. In short, the presence of corporate America was greater than it used to be some thirty years ago, but the character of those few blocks that was carved during the 1960s and 1970s remains as its essence despite numerous attempts by city and university officials and businessmen and women to convert the strip into just another pedestrian mall.

The politics expressed on t-shirts for sale and in posters pasted on fences and shop windows were less radical then I remember. Indeed, the overwhelming number of Obama images was a bit of a surprise to me, especially when compared to the very small number of posters reacting to the ongoing Israeli invasion of Gaza and massacre of Palestinian children. Yet, the most interesting juxtaposition of political imagery appeared in a shop window that featured a poster of Obama and several leaflets calling for protests against the murder of a young black man by the BART transit police. For those of you who don't know, the facts of this case are these. Early New Year's morning an argument on a BART train erupted into a fight. Several passengers involved in the fight were removed from he train at Oakland' Fruitvale station. Several transit police took those involved off the train, cuffed some of them and forced them all to squat near a wall in the station. One young man, named Oscar Grant, was lying face down on the station floor with his hands behind is back when a police officer took out his gun and shot him. He died several hours later. This is my interpretation of the events derived from viewing at least two cellphone videos taken by other passengers and posted on the internet. It is an interpretation shared by thousands of other (if not millions) viewers. In fact, it is the opinion apparently held by the prosecutor involved in the case, as the officer was indicted for murder and turned himself in January 14th, 2009.

The reaction on the street to Grant's murder was definite and quick. People around the Bay Area saw the video and saw murder. Protests were organized by a variety of groups, including churches and radical political sects. The first protest on January 7th attracted a thousand or so people and ended with a small riot in downtown Oakland and the arrest of more than a hundred protesters. Most people were not just angry about the murder, but also that no charges or arrests had been made in the case even though a week had passed since the shooting.

Then there is Barack Obama. If the state of black America could be summed up with the life of one individual, which of these men would we choose to represent that state? Barack Obama, who will become president of the United States on January 20th, 2009, or Oscar Grant, whose life was ended by a police bullet on January 1st, 2009? The very fact of Grant's death shows the world that there is no post-racial America. In fact, it reminds us all that, despite the gains in the area of race in the United States, Barack Obama is the significant exception to the rule. This fact is not a denial of the hopes his election has raised for African-Americans and the nation, but it is a cold reminder that making a black man president is a long way from ending the very real fact of the systemic racism that made this nation what it is. The death of Oscar Grant, like the presence of so many African-Americans in the US prison system, is an even harsher reminder of how that racism plays itself out in the daily lives of so many of its citizens.

Racism will end in this country when it no longer serves the interests of the elites that run it. The presence of a black family in the White House may be a symbolic victory for the forces opposed to racism, but the men and women chosen by Obama to help him rule represent the real nature of his presidency. Malcolm X once said that "An integrated cup of coffee isn't sufficient pay for four hundred years of slave labor." Well, neither is a black man in the White House sufficient enough to forget the death of Oscar Grant and the many other African-Americans whose lives have been destroyed by the very system now governed by Mr. Obama.

Afterword: October 2010. Nothing much has changed since Mr. Obama took office. The war in Afghanistan is bloodier than before and Washington still insists it can be won. At what cost nobody is saying. Unemployment remains high. Wall Street continues to exist in its magical land that seems to have very little to do with the realities of life on Main Street. The Democrats pretend that they are the party of progressive change while the Republicans and their tea partying first cousins fuck not only each other but a certain portion of the electorate who could easily become the modern day version of those American citizens who supported the All-American fascist Buzz Windrip in Sinclair Lewis' 1935 novel *It Can't Happen Here.*

As if to prove the point that little changes in the United States no matter who is in the White House, I include the following piece written in March 2011.

To the Shores of Tripoli

It seems reasonable to state that the reason
Washington launched its machinery of death against
Libya is to insure it would have some input in that
nation's future after Gaddafi's departure. The claim of
saving civilian lives, while laudable, rings as hollow as
ever. As always this claim begs the question how does a
military save civilian lives while destroying civilian
lives? History tells us that this reasoning is only for the
folks watching the attacks on television, not for those in
the region being subjected to them. The Arab League,
having foolishly believed that Washington and NATO
truly exist to save civilian lives, are now regretting their
support of military action in the wake of climbing
civilian casualties. Casualties which the US and its
posse have denied occurring.

While the US and its European cohorts would
probably like to have friendly forces control the entire
country of Libya, they may decide to be content with
those forces in control of the part already held by the
rebels in the east. On February 28, 2011, Abdessalam
Najib, a petroleum engineer at the Libyan company
Agico told a Reuters reporter "Nearly all the oilfields in
Libya east of Ras Lanuf are now controlled by the

people and the government has no control in this area." This area is where a good portion of Libya's major oil fields and related industry are. Of course, should it start looking like the anti-Gaddafi forces find themselves unable to hold that territory, one can be certain Rome, London and Washington will figure out a way to put some friendly troops in there. In fact according to scattered press reports, some from the US may already be there. (reported on WNBI-TV, 3/23/2011, New Bern, NC.)

Beyond Libya lies the greater revolt of the Arab people. Manipulating this revolt and turning the hopes of the people in the region for genuine democracy into a US-style electoral charade seems to be the best Washington can hope for in the near future. For those movements unwilling to settle for this, their battle will become more difficult. It is unlikely that Washington wanted the Egyptian people to go as far as they have. The current situation with the military in control provides some comfort to Washington, but the urgings of the people to move beyond the military has raised concerns. Washington can hardly wait until a government more like Mubarak's is in control. At the same time, Washington's fear is that there will never be another government like that in Cairo. A pro-western military presence in Libya, combined with the repressive regimes in the sheikdoms and Iraq, would certainly help keep a lid on any further revolutionary stirrings. Despite this, even Washington understands (and fears) that revolution operates on its own terms.

The pathetic displays of military hardware combined with the crowing of the Wolf Blitzer-types on cable news channels are nothing new. They shouldn't piss me off like they do. The strutting of that hardware accompanied by statistics about death and capabilities is reminiscent of a football locker room before a game. Without going deeper, suffice it to say that while the aforementioned displays may be pathetic and the crowing by news anchors, the most pathetic displays are those of liberal politicians and their supporters actually believing (for the umpteenth time in the past twenty years) that the US military is doing good. That launching cruise missiles is defending civilians. That Tomahawks and F-22s are something other than the weapons of mass destruction commandeered by uniformed men and women who are essentially cowards. Regarding the other side of the aisle, let me say this. Hearing John Boehner and other Republicans call for the White House to explain to Congress the nature of the mission is a joke. It's not like they have a history of opposing US military intervention or even much affinity for the constitution. Their cries to include Congress are as genuine as Barack Obama's promises to close Gitmo, exit Iraq, and withdraw from Afghanistan by June. On the other hand. what does Obama have to fear by including Congress? It's not like there will be any effective opposition to his imperial foray.

Don't be fooled by the stage managing of this intervention. Just because Robert Gates or General Ham (now is that a name or what?) point to the presence of bombers from Norway, Denmark and even (yes, even) from Qatar, the fact is this is Washington's show. From the halls of Pentagon City to the shores of Tripoli, the power behind the Tomahawks and bombers is all American. And so is the hypocrisy.

Ron Jacobs is, among other things, an anti-imperialist activist and a writer. His articles, essays and reviews appear regularly in *Counterpunch, Dissident Voice* and many other web and print journals. He is the author of *The Way the Wind Blew: a History of the Weather Underground* and the novel *Short Order Frame Up*. His latest novel is titled *The Co-Conspirator's Tale*. He currently lives in Asheville, North Carolina.